Oyster Cookery

Sharon Montoya-Welsh

"He was a bold man that first ate an Oyster."

—*J. Swift*

Oyster Cookery

Sharon Montoya-Welsh

COLLECTORS PRESS

PORTLAND, OREGON

This book is dedicated in memory of my partner, the late Marjorie Speare-Yerxa, without whose inspiration and backing this book would not have been possible.

Permission granted to reprint material from:
The Oysters of Locmariaquer, Eleanor Clark, Pantheon Book, a Division of Random House, Inc., 201 East 50th Street, New York, NY 10022.

Alice's Adventures Through the Looking Glass, Lewis Carroll, Poem: "The Walrus and the Carpenter," MacMillan and Co., Limited, 866 Third Ave., New York, NY 10022.

The Sou'wester, a quarterly publication of the Pacific County Historical Society since 1966, Reprint of: "Raymond's Oyster Money," P.O. Box P, South Bend, WA 98586.

Design: Sara E. Blum
Cover Design: Kevin A. Welsch, Sara E. Blum
Editors: Lindsay S. Brown, Jennifer Weaver-Neist

Distributed by Publisher Group West
ISBN 10: 1-933112-35-2
ISBN 13: 978-1-933112-35-0

Printed in China

9 8 7 6 5 4 3 2 1

All rights reserved
First printing 1984
Second printing 1984

Collectors Press books are available at special discounts for bulk purchases, premiums, and promotions. Special editions, including personalized inserts or covers, and corporate logos, can be printed in quantity for special purposes. For further information contact: Special Sales, Collectors Press, Inc., P.O. Box 230986, Portland, OR 97281. Toll free: 1-800-423-1848.

For a free catalog write to:
Collectors Press, Inc.
P.O. Box 230986
Portland, OR 97281
Toll free: 1-800-423-1848
collectorspress.com

Library of Congress Cataloging-in-Publication Data

Montoya-Welsh, Sharon.
  Oyster cookery / by Sharon Montoya-Welsh & Marjorie Speare-Yerxa. -- 2nd ed.
    p. cm.
  Includes index.
  ISBN 1-933112-35-2 (softcover : alk. paper) 1.
Cookery (Oysters) I. Speare-Yerxa, Marjorie. II. Title.
  TX754.O98M66 2007
  641.6'94--dc22
                2006030550

Table of Contents

Introduction

Let it be said right at the beginning of this book that many oyster connoisseurs claim that there are but four ways to eat oysters—fried, stewed, baked, and raw on the half shell. When I decided to tell the world about this marvelous gift of the sea, however, I couldn't publish a cookbook with only four recipes. So I divided the book into two volumes under one cover: Volume I for the purists and Volume II for the adventurers.

Volume I is presented as a means of keeping tradition alive—especially in places like Oysterville, Washington, where the first printing of *Oyster Cookery* was inspired more than twenty years ago. As the months of the calendar slide away almost unnoticed, so do the landmarks of this old town. People, lifestyles, and architecture change; even the landscape transforms in many ways. It is my hope that this section of the book helps to preserve the original oyster culture that has been so lovingly kept alive by generations of purists, in Oysterville and other places like it.

The purpose of Volume II is to bridge over the time element from the olden days to those of the present. Inspired and created by experimentation with ingredients, methods, and foreign recipe research, modern ways to prepare different dishes are introduced in this section. Working on it was a thoroughly enjoyable endeavor, and I wonder what the next *Oyster Cookery* book will reveal. Let's pray that it will not be oysters in pill form, even if they do resemble pearls.

Did you know?

Every now and then you will come across little items called "Did you know?" I decided to scatter scientific facts and literary points of interest throughout the book instead of producing a theme paper on the subjects. By the time you have read this book, you should know quite a bit about oysters and their legends, and you may even contribute some new ones yourself.

Thoughts on Cookery

Cookery is one of the most ancient and fundamental of the arts. The issue of whether one should live to eat is a question that the epicure and ascetic will truly argue. That one must eat to live, however, is scarcely an opinion but rather a fact.

The creation of a recipe and its presentation stand in the same category as the canvas does to the painter. Be an artist; create and present a meal so delicious and nutritious that you will be repaid a thousand-fold for your work by the enthusiastic praise of those who are fortunate to dine at your table. It is especially satisfying to learn the nutritional values with which you are dealing and how you are contributing to the healthy future of your family and yourself. When preparing a meal, only the freshest of ingredients should be used. Fresh herbs, spices, and vegetables will always enhance your cooking.

Your creative ability as a cook lives on and on after the meal is finished. That is the reason I have decided to write a cookbook—my recipes are passed on. Hopefully, you will take the initiative to create in your own kitchen as well. Use these recipes as a guide to your own creative ability.

A Taste of the Place: Shoalwater Kitchen

O ne day I suddenly realized that fate (I prefer to call it fortune) found me in the glorious land of plenty—plenty of oysters, that is. There are tons of them at the bottom of Shoalwater Bay, now referred to as Willapa Bay, in the village of Oysterville, Washington. My past writing partner, Marge (now deceased), resided "downtown," adjacent to the many oyster beds on Willapa Bay. I lived in "rural" Oysterville, where my husband, Carlos, built us a beautiful home, later to become "Shoalwater Kitchen" and where I eventually taught cooking classes. It was there the original *Oyster Cookery* spawned.

As Marge and I launched into our research and cooking, it became obvious that the role of the fresh, canned, frozen, and smoked oyster should be seriously considered. Oyster tasters were invited to weekly tastings of, believe it or not, several courses of oysters in all forms! Some recipes just did not work, but those that did received the highest rating and made it into this book.

There are a few important things to remember when preparing oysters. Do not overcook them, as they will become rubbery and tasteless. When cooking them in a pot or skillet, be sure to heat or cook only until the edges begin to curl and the oysters are just plump. If purchased in the shell, scrub the shell clean, then proceed to shuck, steam, or barbecue. When serving raw, open with care and do not rinse the inside, thus losing the wonderful oyster liquor. When steaming or barbecuing, cook only until the shells start to pop open or "spit" when lightly tapped. And there is never any need to clean the oyster; the entire thing is edible (except for the shell, of course).

Oysters lend themselves to all sorts of settings. They grace an elegant formal dinner and are great for brunch, lunch, or the traditional beach barbecue. Their gustatorial delight is easily increased by serving complementary side dishes, condiments, and beverages. I offer suggestions, but of course, you are on your own to decide what pleases you.

In the past 20 years, my goal has not changed. All I want is for everyone to love oysters, and I will do my best with *Oyster Cookery* to show you how.

VOLUME I:
The Oyster Purist

About Oysterville

This is the legend that has been passed down through generations about the founding of Oysterville, Washington. In 1851 Mr. R. H. Espy, while visiting the Palix River area with the intention of homesteading there, met an old Indian, Chief Na-Ka-Ti, who told him of great oyster beds across the bay on the Peninsula. An agreement was made that Mr. Espy would return to the place the following year and that Chief Na-Ka-Ti would show him the beds. During the winter, Mr. Espy met Mr. I. A. Clark, and they became good friends and partners. Mr. Espy told Mr. Clark about the oysters, and in early April they set out to find them. While paddling down the bay toward the proposed meeting place, a dense fog descended upon the area. The men got lost, but before they could begin to despair, they heard a muffled pounding sound and proceeded toward it. When they came ashore, they saw their Indian friend pounding on a hollow log. He had seen the two men coming before the fog set in and was trying to guide them to shore. Espy and Clark found the oyster beds of which Na-Ka-Ti had spoken, and platted the town site of Oysterville in 1854, near the beds.

There have been many books and articles written about Oysterville, the Long Beach Peninsula, the Indians, and the oyster industry itself. I have read many of the historical accounts of the early explorers, settlers, and traders of the late 1700s and the 1800s, and I am continually delighted to have felt the close kinship of living in Oysterville.

The journal of James Swan tells us of the early wild animal population, great flocks of birds of many varieties, and the numerous sea and bay creatures that abounded around Shoalwater Bay. These all contributed to the food chain for the wildlife and made the survival of the Indians and settlers possible.

Mr. Swan's book, *The Northwest Coast*, is a must for those who are interested in the early life on Washington's coast. R. H. Espy's grandson, Mr. Willard R. Espy, wrote a book entitled *Oysterville: Roads to Grandpa's Village*, published by Clarkson N. Potter, Inc. of New York. It is a most remarkably researched and thoroughly enjoyable chronicle of Oysterville and is still referenced today by residents and visitors alike.

Did you know?

In 1855 there were employed in the oyster trade in the Bay one schooner of 40 tons, capable of carrying 600 baskets of oysters; 28 boats capable of carrying 2200 baskets of oysters; 21 scows capable of carrying 1980 baskets of oysters; and 13 canoes, capable of carrying 670 baskets of oysters; a total of 5450 baskets of oysters. From 1851–1864, the method of collecting oysters was done by tonging, raking, and hand picking. Only the mature oyster ready for market was taken from the natural bed. Until 1860, much of this work was done by Indians, who were paid in staples—tobacco and whiskey at the rate of twenty-five cents a basket. Although the native oysters in Shoalwater Bay were a staple food of the Indians for hundreds of years, they were not discovered by the white man until the middle of the nineteenth century.

—Oystering in Willapa Bay - Timberline Regional Library
Bibliography: History of Native Oysters - Thesis, Ronald Minks, 1971
Washington State Department of Fisheries - Clyde Sayce

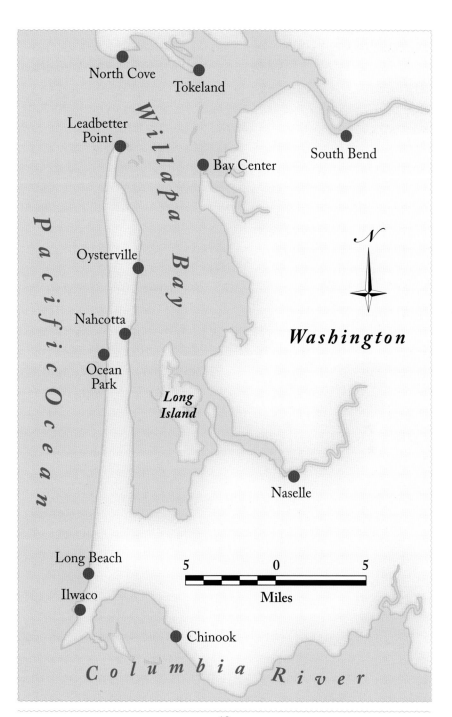

North Cove

Tokeland

Leadbetter Point

Willapa Bay

South Bend

Bay Center

Pacific Ocean

Oysterville

Nahcotta

Ocean Park

Long Island

N

Washington

Naselle

Long Beach

Ilwaco

5   0   5

Miles

Chinook

Columbia River

Oysterville Fried Oysters

*Perfectly fried oysters are plump and juicy with a lovely coating, but
there is a secret to making them this way. After dipping the oysters in an
egg wash and coating them with either flour or finely ground crackers, let
them sit for at least 30 minutes to dry before frying. Your favorite salad,
French bread, french fries, and berry pie make fine accompaniments, and
a good stout or ale is best for washing it all down.*

Serves 4

1 pint shucked oysters (allow 6 per person)
1 cup fine dry bread crumbs or all-purpose flour
Salt and pepper
Garlic powder (optional)
Onion powder (optional)
2 large eggs
1 tablespoon cold water or lemon juice
2 tablespoons butter
2 tablespoons oil

1. Place the oysters in a strainer to drain, reserving the liquor, if desired.
   Set aside.

2. In a small, shallow bowl, season the bread crumbs with salt and
   pepper, then add the garlic powder and onion powder, if using.
   Set aside.

3. Beat the eggs with the cold water in a small bowl.

4. Dip each oyster in the egg wash, then in the seasoned bread crumbs,
   and place it on a baking sheet to dry for 30 to 60 minutes or more.

5. In a medium skillet, melt the butter. Add the oil and heat over medium heat until hot but not smoking. Place the oysters in the skillet and fry, turning once, until golden brown and the edges are curled, about 3 minutes on each side. Do not overcook or overcrowd.

6. Put the fried oysters on paper towels to absorb excess oil and keep warm until all the oysters have been fried. Serve immediately.

TIP: Serve fried oysters with Shoalwater Tartar Sauce (page 149) or Shoalwater Cocktail Sauce (page 151). Fresh lemon wedges are also excellent.

Did you know?

Starting in 1850, large numbers of native oysters were harvested in Shoalwater Bay and shipped live to San Francisco markets.

Oyster Stew

This is the basic but soul-warming recipe for oyster stew. Most households have their own secret ingredient to make the stew taste just like the stew Mother used to make, but those variations have been saved for further discussion in Volume II (page 78). Though this is a simple recipe, be careful not to boil the milk, and do not overcook the oysters.

Serves 4

6 tablespoons butter
1 pint shucked oysters (preferably small)
1 quart milk or half-and-half
Salt and pepper
1 to 2 dashes of paprika

1. Preheat the oven to 250°F.

2. In a medium saucepan, melt 2 tablespoons of butter and sauté the oysters in their liquor until plump and the edges curl. Remove from heat and set aside.

3. Heat the milk over medium heat in a separate medium saucepan. Do not boil.

4. Combine the oysters and juices with the milk, season with salt and pepper, to taste, and keep very warm.

5. Meanwhile, heat the bowls in the oven.

6. Divide the stew equally among the bowls and top each with 1 tablespoon of butter. Sprinkle the tops with paprika and serve hot.

TIP: Oyster stew makes an excellent lunch served with toast or oyster crackers. For a hearty supper, serve the stew with crusty bread and a sliced tomato salad followed by a deep-dish apple pie.

Raw Oysters in the Shell

Raw oysters in the shell can be found at most coastal seafood markets and at inland estuaries, where they are farmed. They are usually sold by the dozen or by the bushel. The following pointers will help you with purchasing, preparing, and enjoying this unique delicacy.

Purchasing

When purchasing fresh oysters, look for tightly closed shells. Partially open shells are not fresh and should be avoided. If you purchase jarred oysters be sure to check the expiration date.

Storing

Store fresh oysters in the refrigerator—or at 40°F—if they are not going to be used immediately. When properly stored, they can be kept up to five days before using.

Cleaning

The outer shell should be scrubbed to remove excess sand, algae, and other debris. This can be done easily with a scrub brush, running water, and elbow grease.

Shucking or Opening

Shucking or opening oysters may seem impossible at first, but a little practice using the proper equipment makes it a manageable task. You should definitely have an oyster knife, a towel or rubber glove, and a plate on which to place the oyster while opening. Two opening methods follow.

Method One

1. Place the live oyster on a plate or on the table with the deep side down and the top (flat side) up.

2. With a towel wrapped around your hand, place your hand on top and around the oyster.

3. Insert an oyster knife between the shells, then twist the knife to loosen the shells and find the best place for inserting the knife fully (pressure is required).

4. Slide the knife along the shell to sever the abductor muscle.

5. Pull the shells apart.

Method Two

This method is generally used to open smaller oysters. It can be done with the oyster resting on the table or held in your hand, with a towel protecting your hand from the knife and the sharp edges of the shell.

1. Position the top (flat side) of the oyster so that it is facing you.

2. Place the knife in the opening at the tip (hinge) of the oyster, and twist the knife to loosen the shells.

3. Insert the knife and slide it away from you along the shell to sever the abductor muscle.

4. Pull the shells apart.

Once you have opened the oyster shell, using either method one or two, cut the bottom muscle and check for pieces of loose shell. If there is shell or sand debris, remove the grit with a clean finger. Running the oyster under water is not recommended, as it tends to remove the delicious liquor.

Serving

Raw oysters on the half shell must be very fresh, very cold, and preferably small. When served at the table, they are usually placed in a large soup plate or on a bed of cracked ice.

The oysters on the half shell (4 to 6 per serving depending on size) are arranged in a circle surrounding a glass jigger or other similar container containing the cocktail sauce. Have additional hot pepper sauce, such as Tabasco, horseradish, and lemon wedges available to apply individually if desired.

Freezing

If you have purchased a great number of oysters in the shell and are not going to use them immediately, you have the option of shucking and freezing them. Use frozen oysters in recipes that call for chopped oysters or that have other ingredients, as freezing does cause flavor loss. Here is a shucking shortcut for freezing.

1. Preheat the oven to 450°F.

2. Place the oysters on a baking sheet and bake for 5 minutes. This causes the abductor muscle to relax while not actually cooking the oyster.

3. Remove the oysters from the oven and let them cool for 5 minutes.

4. Place the deep side of the oyster shell down on a plate so that the flat side is facing up.

5. With a towel in one hand over the oyster and the oyster knife in the other, insert the oyster knife between the shells, twist, and slide the knife across the shell edge to sever the muscle.

6. Open the oyster over the plate to catch all liquor that may escape.

7. Place enough oysters in a freezer container to fill it up halfway.

8. Strain the oyster liquor through fine cheese cloth or a towel into the container until the oysters are covered with the liquor.

9. Cool to room temperature, then cover the container with a lid and place in the freezer. Keep the oysters frozen until you are ready to heat and use them in recipes. Do not freeze longer than 6 months.

Accompaniments

Chilled dry white Chablis, Brut Champagne, or Muscadet wine complements oysters on the half shell. Tiny, spicy, pork link sausages also provide a nice contrast of tastes to the fresh oysters. Serve the sausages hot alongside cold fresh oysters.

Did you know?

Shoalwater Bay, now Willapa Bay, produces 56-percent of the oysters in the state of Washington. Washington state grows 81-percent of all the oysters produced by the Pacific Coast states.

—Pacific Coast Shellfish Growers Association

Fire-Baked Oysters

These oysters are cooked in their shells and served in a fashion that truly creates a day to remember. An oyster barbecue party is apt to last for hours and hours, with music and games contributing to great fun for all ages. Just make sure the oysters are plentiful, very fresh, and kept properly chilled at about 40°F until cooking. Then grill in your own backyard, at a favorite picnic site, or over a driftwood fire and grate at the beach. Corn-on-the-cob, all salads, and homemade bread make excellent accompaniments on the menu.

Serves a crowd

Oysters (at least 6 to 10 per person)
Garlic Butter Sauce (page 156)

1. Wash and scrub the oyster shells.

2. Place the unopened oysters, deep side down, directly on the grate over a charcoal or wood fire. The oysters simmer in their own liquor and are done when the shells begin to open.

3. Using tongs or gloves, remove the oysters from the fire. Carefully (they are hot) open the oysters with an oyster knife. If the deep side of the shell is on the bottom, you will not lose the flavorful juices inside.

4. Serve the oysters hot in their bottom shells with the Garlic Butter Sauce for dipping.

Oven-Baked Oysters

If you are an apartment dweller or must be inside because of rain or other reasons, cooking oysters in the shell is still delicious if done properly in the oven. This recipe incorporates a layer of rock salt to distribute the temperature evenly and prevent the oysters from tilting when baking.

Serves a crowd

Oysters (at least 6 to 10 per person)
Rock salt (optional)
Sauce(s) of choice (pages 145–157)

1. Preheat the oven to 450°F.

2. Wash and scrub the oyster shells.

3. Place the oysters, deep side down, on a baking sheet covered with a 1/4- to 1/2-inch layer of rock salt, if using.

4. Bake the oysters for about 12 to 15 minutes, until the shells begin to open.

5. Remove the oysters from the oven. Carefully (they are hot) open the oysters with an oyster knife. If the deep side of the shell is on the bottom, you will not lose the flavorful juices inside.

6. Serve the oysters hot in their bottom shells with a sauce alongside for dipping.

"It's a Sex Problem"

If at first the conversation at your party is a little strained, here are some interesting and vital morsels of interest to interject and start the ball rolling—after you have passed the hors d'oeuvres, of course.

Mr. Doug Welch had this to say about oyster breeding in the *Seattle Post-Intelligencer* article "Oyster in a Stew; It's a Sex Problem":

In the spring a young oyster's fancy turns lightly toward thoughts of love—and about one hundred twenty million offspring each.

But along the time of year when fall spreads its soft mantle everywhere, a young oyster spends most of his time wondering whether he is (1) a little boy oyster, or (2) a little girl oyster.

He never knows, when he arises in the morning, whether he ought to slip into trousers or into a silk print dress.

Further information on this subject is provided by the late zoology professor Trevor Kincaid of the University of Washington.

It's strictly a case of Dr. Jekyll and Mrs. Hyde. This is particularly true of the native oyster, which is bisexual. Last spring these little fellows were sitting around talking baseball and politics. Now they are all knitting on tiny garments. Come winter and they'll slip into a comfortable state of quietude in which they're neither Ned nor Nancy.

The Japanese oyster, on the other hand, may be either a male or a female for several years running. But the males invariably turn into females along about the fourth year and there is nothing they can do about it. Struggle as they may against it, sooner or later they all appear in public with roses in their teeth.

VOLUME II:
The Oyster Adventurer

Oysterville Today

The sign at the fork in the road still reads "Oysterville 1854," and yes, Oysterville is still a sleepy little village. However, returning twenty years later, I am immediately struck by the growth, not of the town, but of the trees and foliage. The red cottage once belonging to local author Willard Espy is no longer in blatant view of the neighboring house, which stirred quite the commotion among the townspeople when it was constructed some fifteen years earlier.

Along the main street, several recently built homes pleasantly blend in with the surroundings. Historic houses remain intact, with several showing their age, perhaps neglected by "nonresidents." The red-steepled church has been impeccably maintained, and Sunday vesper services are still held in the summer months. Likewise, the old school house has been restored, serving as a community center, and is host to the popular Jazz & Oysters festival held on its lawn in late August.

Bayside, the historic Northern Oyster Company cannery, which had been on the verge of crumbling in the next sou'wester, has been restored and renamed Oysterville Sea Farms. It now functions as the last surviving oyster operation in town. Dan Driscoll, a self-described "old school" oysterman, acquired the family business, refurbished the cannery, and now runs a bustling seafood outlet and gift shop, where one can purchase oysters along with other delicacies.

A final walk up the hill to the Oysterville Store and Post Office, where locals still receive their daily mail, was like a journey through time that had stood still. Proprietors John and Jeanne Smith welcomed my husband and I with open arms, and we chatted about old times.

Continuing through "rural" Oysterville to the original site of Shoalwater Kitchen, we saw that little has changed beyond a few new signs directing the way to Leadbetter State Park, now accessible by paved road. In the past, a pick-up truck was the more reliable mode of transportation.

Despite small changes and time, it is comforting to know that Oysterville is still an enchanting place to visit.

Hors d'oeuvres & Appetizers

Hors d'oeuvres and appetizers are generally served with drinks before a main meal. Literally translated, hors d'oeuvre means "outside the main works," and should have distinct piquant flavors served in small portions to whet, not satisfy, the appetite. If one is simply having a cocktail party, however, platters full of delicious hors d'oeuvres and appetizers should be set out while guests are enjoying their libations.

Smoked Oysters with Lemon on Toast

These little nuggets of flavor seem to instantly disappear when served with your favorite drink (preferably a chilled bottle of Champagne). Life becomes truly festive, and it is all so easy. Be sure to make plenty, as they make excellent hors d'oeuvres for a party.

Makes 12

1 loaf sliced sandwich bread
2 medium lemons
4 tablespoons (1/2 stick) butter
1 (3-ounce) can smoked oysters, drained
Fresh parsley sprigs, to serve

1. With a round 2-inch cookie cutter, cut rounds out of the sliced bread, omitting the crusts. You should be able to get 3 rounds out of each slice. Set aside.

2. Use a very sharp knife to slice the lemons paper thin, rind and all. Then cut the slices in half and set aside.

3. Melt 3 tablespoons of butter in a large skillet over medium-high heat. Fry the bread rounds on both sides until they are nicely browned; do not overcrowd the pan. Remove the finished rounds from the skillet and place on a platter. Repeat with the remaining rounds, frying in batches and adding more butter if necessary.

4. Place a lemon slice on each toast round and top with a single smoked oyster.

5. Arrange the rounds on a serving platter garnished with the parsley and serve.

For the Hors d'oeuvre Platter

Canned smoked oysters may be found at almost any grocery store, and local fish stores usually offer fresh smoked oysters. There are many ways in which these tiny delicacies may be prepared and enjoyed. Serve as an appetizer or as a first course with one of the following three ingredients or combinations. They make delicious and quick appetizers and do not require toothpicks or forks. And it is perfectly proper to serve them at room temperature, as no cooking is required.

Note: Canned smoked oysters are very oily.
Drain before using and discard the oil.

Serves a crowd

Cheese and crackers: Arrange your favorite cheese and crackers on a round serving platter. Put the smoked oysters in a separate bowl and place the bowl in the center of the platter, with a serving fork available.

Cherry tomatoes: Slice off the tops of the cherry tomatoes and scoop out a little of the inside. Place a drained, smoked oyster in each tomato. Garnish with fresh parsley, and if desired, top with lemon juice. Serve on a bed of lettuce with lemon wedges as a first course. A full platter also makes an attractive cocktail hors d'oeuvre.

Fresh mushrooms: Wipe the mushrooms clean with a damp towel and pull out the stems. Place a drained, smoked oyster in each mushroom. Garnish with a sprig of parsley and sprinkle with lemon juice if desired. Create a bed of lettuce on a serving platter and arrange the stuffed mushrooms on top to serve.

"Which he ate up all, he found them so appetizing."
—François Rabelais

Smoked Oyster Dip

This recipe is an automatic surprise wherever it appears. It is delicious and unique with crackers, potato chips, or fresh raw vegetables.

Makes about 1 cup

1 (12-ounce) package cream cheese, softened
1 (3-ounce) can smoked oysters with oil
3 drops hot pepper sauce, such as Tabasco
3 dashes of onion powder
2 to 3 tablespoons dry sherry (optional)

1. Put all the ingredients into a blender and blend until smooth.

2. Place in a serving bowl and chill until ready to serve.

*"Appetite comes with eating—
but the thirst goes away with drinking."*
—*Françios Rabelais*

Cocktail Oysters

*These unique, spicy–tart morsels speak for themselves, and
they do not require much preparation. Serve them with toothpicks
and cocktails. A variation follows.*

Note: This recipe must be prepared a day ahead of time.

Serves 6

1 quart shucked oysters (preferably small)
Dry white wine, as needed
5 whole cloves or allspice berries
10 whole black peppercorns
1/4 cup lemon juice
1 medium lemon, thinly sliced
Dash of hot pepper sauce, such as Tabasco

1. In a medium saucepan, poach the oysters in their liquor over medium
   heat until plump, approximately 5 to 8 minutes. The liquor should
   completely cover the oysters while poaching. If more liquid is needed
   add up to 1/2 cup of white wine till covered.

2. Remove the oysters from the pan using a slotted spoon. Place them in
   a large bowl and set aside.

3. In the same saucepan with the reserved oyster liquor, add the cloves,
   peppercorns, lemon juice, lemon slices, and hot pepper sauce. Bring to
   a slight boil and simmer for 15 minutes.

4. Remove the pan from the heat and pour the hot marinade over the
   oysters. Refrigerate the oysters in their marinade for at least 24 hours.

5. Drain the oysters and serve well chilled.

Cocktail Oysters in Sour Cream Sauce

Complete the recipe for Cocktail Oysters (page 43) as directed. After the oysters have marinated for at least 12 hours, place them in the following additional sauce. This is an attractive first course when care is taken to arrange the oysters, onion rings, and thinly sliced lemons on individual plates.

Serves 6

1 recipe of Cocktail Oysters (page 43)
1 (16-ounce) container sour cream, plus more if serving as a first course
1 tablespoon plus 1/2 teaspoon prepared horseradish
1 medium white onion, thinly sliced into rings
1 to 2 medium lemons, thinly sliced
Toast rounds (optional)
Lettuce, for serving (optional)
1 medium lemon, thinly sliced (optional)

1. Drain the marinated cocktail oysters, reserving the marinade. Set aside.

2. In a medium bowl, mix the sour cream, horseradish, and half of the onion rings. If the mixture is too thick, dilute it with 1 tablespoon of the reserved marinade.

3. Add the drained oysters to the sour cream mixture, making sure they are covered. Chill for at least 4 hours.

4. For an hors d'oeuvre, serve the oysters and sauce well-chilled on toast rounds. As a first course, make a bed of lettuce on individual plates, and arrange 3 oysters including a few of the remaining onion rings and a dollop of sour cream per serving. Garnish the plates with a slice of lemon, if using.

Sherry-Marinated Raw Oysters

Duplicate the recipe as needed for this pleasing appetizer.
Count on at least six oysters per person.

Serves 1

6 small oysters, shucked
2 tablespoons dry sherry
Pinch of salt
Dash of cayenne pepper
Fresh parsley sprigs, to serve

1. In a medium bowl, sprinkle the oysters with the sherry, salt, and cayenne pepper, and gently mix.

2. Refrigerate the mixture for at least 30 minutes before serving. Have oyster forks or toothpicks handy and garnish with the parsley.

Did you know?

The International Federation of World Eating cites Virginian Sonya "The Black Widow" Thomas as the 2005 world champion in oyster eating. On March 20, 2005, at the Acme Oyster House in New Orleans, Sonya ate 46 dozen oysters in 10 minutes. This amounts to about 55 oysters per minute. She gets her nickname from her amazing ability to triumph over men who are four to five times larger than her. Wow!

Brunch & Lunch

This section offers many ideas as to what to serve to guests at brunch or lunchtime. Most of the recipes are quick and very easy to prepare. If fresh oysters are not at hand, always keep a supply of canned or smoked oysters. They will serve you well!

Oysters From Boston

Although this recipe originated in Boston, it made a cross-country trip in high fashion, never tangling with Rocky Mountain oysters! Serve as a first course, allowing two medium oysters per person. When served as a main course, allow at least four medium oysters per person. Serve with rice pilaf, a vegetable, and chilled Muscadet wine.

Makes 12

3 scallions, minced
1 1/2 teaspoons minced fresh tarragon
1 1/2 teaspoons chervil
1/3 cup fine dry bread crumbs
1/2 cup (1 stick) butter
Salt, to taste
Dash of hot pepper sauce, such as Tabasco
12 medium oysters, shucked
Rock salt (optional)
Pernod or anisette liqueur

1. Preheat the oven to 425°F.

2. In a medium bowl, combine the scallions, tarragon, chervil, bread crumbs, butter, salt, and hot pepper sauce. Blend until a smooth paste is achieved and set aside.

3. Place the oysters in deep oyster shells, ramekins, or a baking dish. Stabilize the shells (if using) with a 1/4-inch to 1/2-inch layer of rock salt on a baking sheet.

4. Spoon 1 tablespoon or more of the bread crumb mixture over each oyster and sprinkle with a dash of Pernod.

5. Bake approximately 8 minutes, until the tops begin to brown. Serve hot in the shells or dishes they are baked in.

Leadbetter Oysters with Sherry

Looking for something easy but elegant to prepare when unexpected guests arrive? Give them a taste of the sea by serving this pleasing appetizer. If serving as a first course, offer dry sherry as the apéritif.

Serves 6

1 pint shucked oysters (preferably small)
2 tablespoons butter
1/2 cup finely chopped celery
2 tablespoons finely chopped green bell pepper
1 tablespoon chopped scallions
1/2 teaspoon salt
1/2 teaspoon paprika
Freshly ground black pepper
1/2 cup dry sherry or Madeira wine
Hot buttered toast slices
Fresh parsley sprigs, to serve

1. Drain the oysters and discard the liquor. Set the oysters aside.

2. In a medium skillet, melt the butter over medium heat. Add the celery and bell pepper and sauté until soft, about 3 minutes. Mix in the scallions, salt, paprika, black pepper, to taste, and the oysters. Cook until the oysters are plump and their edges begin to curl. Do not overcook.

3. Pour the sherry into the skillet and keep well heated until ready to serve.

4. Place a few oysters on each toast slice with a spoonful of the sauce over each portion. Garnish with the parsley and serve.

Oysters in White Wine Sauce

The presentation and flavor of this recipe is perfect for a midmorning or midday meal. Served in the shell with a garlic–wine marinade, these oysters can be simply accompanied by slices of French bread and an endive salad, topped with your favorite dressing. A more decadent variation using bacon follows.

Serves 3

Marinade:
1 cup dry white wine
1/2 teaspoon minced garlic
1/4 cup minced fresh parsley
Freshly ground black pepper

Oysters:
1 pint shucked oysters, drained (fresh or jarred)
Rock salt (optional)
Oyster shells (optional)
Butter
Fine dry bread crumbs
1/4 cup minced fresh parsley

1. Preheat the oven to 400°F.

2. In a medium bowl, combine the white wine, garlic, parsley, and black pepper, to taste.

3. Place the shucked oysters in the marinade and refrigerate for 1 hour.

4. Line a baking sheet with a 1/4- to 1/2-inch layer of rock salt. This helps to stabilize the oyster shells and distribute temperature evenly. (Note: If shells are not available, individual ramekins or a shallow casserole dish will do, and rock salt would not be required.)

5. Place 1 marinated oyster or several small oysters in the deep side of an oyster shell. Place the shell on the bed of rock salt and repeat until all the oysters have been used. Do not discard the remaining marinade.

6. Pour 1 tablespoon of marinade over each oyster, top each oyster with 1/4 tablespoon of butter, then sprinkle the tops lightly with bread crumbs.

7. Bake approximately 8 minutes or until the oysters are plump and the edges are curled.

8. Remove the oysters from the oven. Garnish each with minced parsley and serve hot in the shells.

Bacon-Cheese Oysters in White Wine Sauce: Before baking Oysters in White Wine Sauce, top the oysters with crumbled bacon or cheese or both. Serve in oyster shells individually or serve on toast points or fried bread rounds. Chilled white wine is an excellent accompaniment.

If you don't love life, you can't enjoy an oyster. You are eating the sea, that's it; only the sensation of a gulp of seawater has been wafted out of it by some sorcery and on the verge of remembering you don't know what, mermaids or a sudden smell of kelp on the ebb tide or a poem you once read, something connected with the flavor of life itself.
—Eleanor Clark

Oysters Rockefeller

There are many versions of this popular oyster preparation, with its spinach-cream sauce and touch of flavored liqueur. This is my take on it, with a variation following this recipe. For an added twist, sprinkle freshly grated Parmesan cheese over the oysters before baking.

Serves 4

Rock salt
1 pound spinach or 1 (1-pound) bag frozen spinach
1 scallion, finely chopped
Juice of 1 medium lemon
2 tablespoons butter
2 tablespoons all-purpose flour
1/2 cup half-and-half, warmed
Dash of nutmeg
Dash of paprika
Dash of cayenne pepper
Dash of salt
Freshly ground black pepper
12 medium oysters, shucked, shells reserved
Pernod or anisette
Fine dry bread crumbs

1. Preheat the oven to 475°F.

2. Line a baking sheet with a 1/4- to 1/2-inch layer of rock salt and set aside.

3. If using fresh spinach, wash the leaves, remove and discard the stems, and steam in a medium saucepan over boiling water until wilted. Drain and chop. If using frozen spinach, thaw, squeeze out the excess liquid, and chop.

4. Add the scallions and lemon juice to the pan and set aside.

5. In the top of a double boiler, melt the butter over medium-low heat. Add the flour and whisk until smooth. Slowly add the warm half-and-half and blend. Mix in the nutmeg, paprika, cayenne pepper, salt, and ground black pepper. Reduce the heat to low, and cook, stirring constantly, until thick.

6. Combine the spinach mixture and cream sauce in the double boiler and remove from heat.

7. Lay the deep side of the oyster shells on the bed of rock salt and spoon 2 rounded tablespoons of creamed spinach into each shell. Place an oyster or oysters (depending on size) on each spoonful of spinach and pour 1/2 teaspoon Pernod over each portion. Top with fine dry breadcrumbs.

8. Bake approximately 10 minutes, until the tops start to brown. Serve hot in the shells.

Oysters Rockefeller with Green Pepper: Sauté 1 tablespoon finely chopped green bell pepper in butter until soft. Prepare the spinach mixture in Oysters Rockefeller, mixing in the sautéed bell pepper. Complete the recipe as directed.

Oysters with Cheese and Bacon

When people are uncertain about oysters, this popular recipe often makes oyster lovers of them. If serving as an hors d'oeuvre instead of for brunch or lunch, spear the oysters with toothpicks and arrange them on a serving platter.

Serves 3 to 4

12 small oysters, shucked or jarred
1/2 cup all-purpose flour, seasoned with salt and pepper
1/2 cup fine dry bread crumbs
2 large eggs, lightly beaten
10 ounces sharp Cheddar cheese, sliced
6 thin slices bacon, halved
Toast or fried bread rounds, to serve
Fresh parsley sprigs, to serve
Lemon quarters, to serve

1. Preheat the oven to 400°F.

2. Drain the oysters and pat them dry with paper towels.

3. Arrange the seasoned flour, bread crumbs, and eggs in three separate dishes.

4. Roll an oyster in the flour (shake off any excess), then dip it in the eggs and roll it in the bread crumbs. Place it on a plate and repeat until all the oysters are coated.

5. Wrap each oyster with a slice of cheese and 1/2 slice of bacon and place them, seam side down, on a baking sheet.

6. Bake 7 to 10 minutes or until the bacon is cooked.

7. Place the oysters on toast or fried bread rounds. Arrange the rounds on a serving platter, and garnish with the parsley and quartered lemons. Serve immediately.

Oysters Casino

*Similar to Oysters with Cheese and Bacon, this versatile recipe bakes
and serves a tasty combination right in the shell. A red wine, such as
a California Zinfandel, is a satisfying complement to this recipe's rich,
smoky flavors. And if you enjoy a splurge of oysters, I heartily suggest
following this course with Spanish Chicken-Oyster Casserole (page 100).*

**Note: When fresh oysters are not available, jarred oysters can be used.
Just place the drained oysters side by side in a shallow baking dish,
and omit step 3 and the first part of step 4.**

Serves 3 to 4

12 medium oysters
Rock salt
Shoalwater cocktail sauce (page 151)
10 ounces sharp Cheddar cheese, sliced
6 thin slices bacon, halved
Freshly ground black pepper
1/2 cup minced fresh parsley

1. Preheat the oven to 400°F.

2. Shuck and drain the oysters, reserving the shells. Set both aside.

3. Spread the rock salt in a 1/4-inch to 1/2-inch layer on a baking sheet
   to prevent the shells from tipping and losing their contents. Set aside.

4. Put 1 to 2 oysters (depending on size) in each shell and place the shells on
   the bed of rock salt. Top each portion with 1 to 2 tablespoons of cocktail
   sauce, a slice of cheese, 1/2 slice of bacon, and a dash of black pepper.

5. Bake in the oven for 10 to 15 minutes, until the bacon is cooked.

6. Remove the oysters from the oven, sprinkle the tops with the minced
   parsley, and serve in the shells on small plates with forks.

Every day they call and say
"What's going on in Willapa Bay?
Hey, what's going on in the bay today?
When will the Oysters start to lay?
Hey, what do you do up there all day
In your little grey lab on Willapa Bay?
Get to work and earn your pay.
Make the Oysters spawn today!"

Well...For Your Information...

An Oysterman's big and full of brawn,
But he can't make an Oyster spawn.
A biologist's smart (or so they say),
But he can't make an Oyster lay.
So let's abandon biology
And try applied psychology.
The trouble's not salinity,
Nor yet is it chlorinity.
And it's not, (as you've been told)
Because the water's too darn cold.
The trouble with Oysters, if you please,
Is they can't tell the he's from she's.
Separate the boys and girls,
(neuter ones are the ones with pearls).
Take a tip from the birds and bees,
And isolate the she's from he's.
Tuck them in, in separate beds
Where they can lay their little heads.
Mark "his" and "hers" upon a sign

And down the middle, draw a line.
Oysters are just like me and you.
It's lots more fun if it's taboo.
Convince the Oysters that it's wrong
And they'll spawn like crazy, all year long!

—Contributed by Janet McDonald
Washington State Oyster Lab. Nahcotta, Washington, 1980

Oyster Quiche á la Paul Calvert

*Marge's son-in-law, Paul, was known for his fine quiche recipes.
At our request, he experimented with an oyster quiche and was totally
successful on his first try! I can't tell you if it's good cold because there are
never leftovers. A cucumber salad with vinaigrette dressing is a superb
accompaniment to this quiche.*

Serves 4

Pastry:
1 cup plus 3 tablespoons all-purpose flour
3 tablespoons butter
3 1/2 tablespoons vegetable shortening
3 to 5 tablespoons chilled milk

Custard:
1 cup milk
3 large eggs
Dash of cayenne pepper or freshly ground black pepper
Dash of garlic powder

Filling:
2 tablespoons butter
1/4 pound mushrooms, sliced
1 pint shucked oysters (preferably small)
2 scallions, chopped
1 cup shredded mild Cheddar cheese, Swiss, or Gruyère (about 4 ounces)
1/2 cup freshly grated Parmesan cheese

1. To make the pastry, put the flour in a medium bowl and use a pastry
   blender or two knives to cut in the butter and shortening until it has
   the appearance of coarse cornmeal. Add 3 tablespoons of milk and mix
   until the mixture starts forming into a ball. Do not add any more milk
   unless it is absolutely necessary in helping the mixture to stick together.

2. Collect the dough into a fairly loose ball and roll it out on a floured surface into a circle large enough to accommodate a 9-inch pie pan or quiche dish.

3. Grease the pie pan and then gently place the pastry into it, being careful not to stretch or tear the dough. Flute the edges and prick the bottom and sides with a fork, to allow the steam to escape during baking. Set aside.

4. To make the custard, beat the milk, eggs, cayenne pepper, and garlic powder thoroughly in a medium bowl. Do not beat it so well that a thick froth develops. Set aside.

5. Preheat the oven to 350°F.

6. To make the filling, melt the butter in a medium skillet over medium heat. Stir in the sliced mushrooms, then add the oysters and their liquor. Sauté until the oyster edges begin to curl.

7. Pour the oyster mixture into a strainer and set it aside to drain.

8. Spread two-thirds of the scallions in the bottom of the pastry. Add an even layer of the oyster mixture and sprinkle the remaining scallions over the top. Follow with the shredded cheese, then pour the custard over all to within 1/4-inch of the pan's edge. Top it off with an even layer of the grated Parmesan cheese.

9. Bake for 40 to 45 minutes or until the custard is set. You can test this by inserting a knife into the center of the custard. When the knife comes out clean, the custard is done.

10. Cool the quiche on a wire rack for 5 minutes, cut, and serve.

Oysters á la Jay Scott

A rich dish—as was the Duchess Patty Posterior who gave this recipe to former Oysterville resident Jay Scott—this recipe is surprisingly simple. I recommend that it be served only as a first course, accompanied by a fine Chablis.

Serves 2

8 medium oysters, shucked, liquor reserved
1/2 cup heavy cream
2 drops hot pepper sauce, such as Tabasco
4 ounces freshly grated Parmesan cheese (about 1 cup packed)
2 tablespoons dried mint leaves
Sour cream, to serve

1. In a medium skillet, poach the oysters with their liquor until they are plump and their edges curl. Remove the oysters with a slotted spoon and keep them warm.

2. In the same skillet, add the heavy cream and hot pepper sauce to the oyster liquor. Slowly add the Parmesan cheese and reduce the heat to low, stirring continuously, until smooth. Set aside.

3. Place 4 warm oysters on two small plates. Pour the hot cheese sauce over the oysters, and sprinkle them with mint leaves.

4. Top each with a spoonful of sour cream and serve.

Oysters Benedict

For that special Sunday brunch, Oysters Benedict makes a voluptuous main dish. Serve with your favorite Champagne, or add orange juice to Champagne in equal ratios for a sparkling morning treat. Ingredient amounts are flexible to suit the number of guests around your table.

Serves a few or a crowd

Oysters, shucked or jarred (2 per muffin half)
Butter
Thinly sliced ham
Toasted English muffin halves
Hot Hollandaise sauce (page 148)
Minced fresh parsley, to serve

1. Drain the oysters and set aside.

2. Melt a little butter in a large skillet over medium heat. Lightly sauté the ham, then remove it from the pan and keep it warm.

3. In the same skillet over medium heat, melt more butter, if desired, and sauté the oysters until the edges begin to curl. Remove the skillet from the heat and set aside.

4. Place a slice of ham on each English muffin half. Top with 2 oysters, then follow with 2 tablespoons of Hollandaise sauce.

5. Garnish with the minced parsley and serve.

Oysters are the usual opening to a winter breakfast...indeed they are almost indispensable.

—*L'Almanach des Gourmands, 1803*
Grimod de la Reyniére

Oysters in Aspic

Individual molds are needed for this dish, which is quite attractive as a salad course for a summer evening meal. Serve with your favorite Champagne to make any occasion flavorful and special. A variation follows.

Note: This recipe requires overnight preparation.

Makes 8

8 small to medium oysters, shucked, liquor reserved
1 (28-ounce) can whole tomatoes
1 teaspoon salt
1/2 teaspoon paprika
4 1/2 teaspoons sugar
3 tablespoons lemon juice
3 tablespoons chopped onion
2 bay leaves
2 medium celery stalks, finely chopped
1 tablespoon basil
1 teaspoon oregano
Hot pepper sauce, such as Tabasco
2 tablespoons (two 1/4-ounce packages) unflavored gelatin
1/2 cup cold water
Slivered scallions, green parts only, to serve (optional)
Fresh parsley sprigs, to serve (optional)
Black olives, to serve (optional)
Lettuce leaves, to serve
Lemon Mayonnaise, to serve (recipe on following page)

1. In a small saucepan, poach the oysters in their own liquor until their edges curl. Drain and set aside to cool.

2. Place the tomatoes, salt, paprika, sugar, lemon juice, onion, bay leaves, celery, basil, oregano, and hot pepper sauce, to taste, in a large, nonreactive saucepan. Bring the mixture to a boil slowly over medium-low heat. Reduce the heat to low and simmer for 1 hour, stirring occasionally while mashing the ingredients.

3. When the tomato mixture has cooked, strain it through a fine-mesh strainer. Strain twice if the juice is not clear of lumps. You should have approximately 4 cups of tomato juice.

4. Dissolve the gelatin in the cold water, then add it to the tomato juice and stir. Pour the mixture into individual 3-inch molds.

5. Refrigerate until thickened but not set.

6. Push the slivered scallions, parsley, and black olives, if using, into the gelatin in a decorative pattern, along with any other garnishes you might wish to use. In the middle of the mold, set in an oyster, do not push all the way down so that a layer of tomato gelatin closes over the top of the oyster. Refrigerate until firm.

7. Unmold the individual aspic onto plates lined with the lettuce leaves. Serve plain or with lemon mayonnaise.

Lemon Mayonnaise: Add fresh squeezed lemon juice to mayonnaise, adjusting amount to taste.

Easy Oysters in Aspic: If you do not have time to make the homemade tomato juice in the original Oysters in Aspic, simply add gelatin to the canned variety and skip the first 3 steps of the recipe. Add spices and water to the tomato juice as needed [1 tablespoon (one 1/4-ounce packet) of unflavored gelatin will gel 2 cups of liquid], and complete the recipe as directed.

Shoalwater Oysters and Mushrooms on Toast

This recipe is easy to prepare for a quick and delicious luncheon. The quantity can also be doubled with little effort to serve a larger crowd.

Serves 4

2 tablespoons butter
1 tablespoon chopped scallions
1/2 cup thinly sliced onions
1/2 cup sliced mushrooms
1 pint shucked oysters
1 tablespoon minced fresh tarragon
1/2 cup dry white wine
Freshly ground black pepper
4 slices buttered toast

1. Melt the butter in a medium skillet over medium heat. Add the scallions, onions, and mushrooms and sauté until well coated, about 1 minute.

2. Drain the oysters and discard the liquor. Add the oysters to the skillet and sauté 4 minutes or until the oysters plump and the edges curl.

3. Add the tarragon, wine, and black pepper. Continue to cook until the mixture is heated through, about 2 minutes.

4. Remove the skillet from the heat and divide the oyster mixture equally onto the slices of toast. Serve immediately.

Shoalwater Oyster Spinach Crepes

When having Champagne with this course, open a bottle ahead of time, enjoy a glass, and add 1/2 cup to the cream sauce. This will bring life to the sauce (and to you!). Pickled watermelon rind provides a nice accent to the serving plate, and broiled tomatoes add color.

Note: Please read the entire recipe before proceeding, as the order of ingredients, the preparation, and timing are more involved in this one.

Serves 6

Crepes:
2 1/2 tablespoons butter, or more as needed
2 large eggs
1 cup all-purpose flour
1/2 teaspoon salt
1 cup milk

Spinach-oyster filling:
1 pint shucked oysters
2 tablespoons butter
2 pounds spinach or 2 (1-pound) bags frozen spinach
1/2 cup chopped scallions
Salt and pepper
Freshly ground nutmeg

Cream sauce:
3 cups half-and-half or 2 1/2 cups half-and-half mixed
   with 1/2 cup Champagne
6 tablespoons butter
6 tablespoons all-purpose flour
Salt and pepper
Freshly ground nutmeg
3 tablespoons freshly grated Parmesan cheese

1. To make the crepes, melt 2 tablespoons of butter in a small saucepan over medium heat and set aside.

2. In a medium bowl, beat the eggs well, then add the flour, salt, milk, and melted butter. Mix only until blended; do not overmix. Cover the batter and let it chill in the refrigerator for at least 2 hours. The batter should be thin.

3. In a crepe pan or small omelet pan, melt 1/2 tablespoon of butter over medium-high heat. Spoon about 2 tablespoons of batter into the pan. Quickly rotate the pan so that a thin layer of batter covers the entire bottom. Cook a few minutes, then gently turn the crepe over. This is easily done with your fingers. Cook until lightly browned and stack on a plate. Repeat until all the batter is used, adding more butter to the pan as needed. Set the finished crepes aside.

4. To cook the oysters for the spinach-oyster filling, drain the oysters and discard the liquor or reserve for another use.

5. In a medium skillet over medium heat, sauté the oysters in the butter until plump and the edges curl, about 5 to 8 minutes. Drain and set aside to cool.

6. Before completing the filling, proceed with making half of the cream sauce. In a small saucepan, heat 1 1/2 cups of half-and-half over medium heat; do not boil. Remove the pan from the heat and set aside.

7. In a double boiler, melt 3 tablespoons of butter over medium heat. Add 3 tablespoons of flour and whisk for 3 minutes. Slowly add the heated half-and-half and whisk until thick. Add salt, pepper, and nutmeg, to taste, and 1 1/2 tablespoons Parmesan cheese. Stir until blended, then set aside and keep warm.

(continued on next page)

8. To finish making the spinach-oyster filling, steam the fresh spinach in a medium saucepan over boiling water until wilted. Drain and chop. If using frozen spinach, thaw, squeeze out the excess liquid, and chop.

9. In a large bowl, combine the spinach and scallions. Chop the cooked oysters coarsely and add them to the bowl. Pour the warm cream sauce into the bowl and gently mix together. Adjust the salt, pepper, and nutmeg as needed and set aside.

10. Repeat steps 6 and 7 to make the remaining cream sauce and keep warm as directed.

11. Preheat the oven to 375°F and grease a 9 x 11-inch baking dish.

12. To assemble the crepes, put 2 to 3 tablespoons of the spinach-oyster filling in the center of each crepe. Roll up the crepes and place them side by side (seam-side down) in the baking dish.

13. Bake the crepes until they are heated through, about 10 minutes.

14. Place 2 crepes on each plate and top with 1/2 cup of warm cream sauce per serving. Serve immediately.

TIP: This recipe can be prepared ahead of time, but the success of doing this lies in making the cream sauce topping just before serving. Make a half portion of the cream sauce and add it to the spinach-oyster mixture as directed. Arrange the stuffed crepes in a buttered casserole or on an ovenproof platter. Do not proceed with making the remaining cream sauce at this time. Cover the crepes with plastic wrap and place them in the refrigerator until you are ready to heat them. While the crepes are heating in the 375°F oven, make the remaining cream sauce topping and complete the recipe as directed.

Oyster Sandwich

This is a simple yet delicious sandwich for all oyster lovers.
Serve with beer and salad or simply with an
iced tea or a good cup of coffee.

Serves 4

Shoalwater Tartar Sauce (page 149)
Shoalwater Cocktail Sauce (page 151)
8 toasted slices sourdough bread
1 pint fried oysters (page 20)

Spread tartar sauce and cocktail sauce on the sourdough bread slices, as desired, and place about 6 oysters on each sandwich. Serve hot.

Did you know?

According to ancient Roman author and philosopher
Pliny the Elder, artificial oyster beds were first formed at Baiae
by Sergius Orata, a contemporary of Crassus the orator, not for
gratification of gluttony, but as a speculative commercial venture
from which he derived a large income.

Oyster-Hamburger Sandwich

Surprise, surprise! Here is an entry in the popularity contest that always wins! Believe it or not, people who are not keen on oysters really love this sandwich. As an added perk, it is high in protein and tastes great when accompanied by a good strong ale or beer, or even buttermilk, for that matter. For the best results, serve with the "Tomato Shoop" recipe on page 83.

Serves 6

1 pint shucked oysters
1 pound lean ground beef, plus more as needed
1 cup dry bread crumbs, plus more as needed
2 tablespoons beer (preferably dark ale)
1/2 tablespoon freshly ground black pepper
1/2 cup sautéed chopped onions (optional)
Salt
2 tablespoons butter
12 slices French or sourdough bread
Shoalwater Tartar Sauce (page 149)
Sliced tomatoes, to serve
Sliced onions, to serve
Lettuce, to serve

1. Drain the oysters and pat dry with paper towels, reserving the liquor for another use. Coarsely chop the oysters. (Note: Oyster liquor is a delicious addition to soup broths.)

2. In a large bowl, combine the oysters, beef, bread crumbs, 1 tablespoon of beer, black pepper, onions, if using, and salt, to taste. Mix well, preferably with your hands, so you can feel the consistency and more thoroughly incorporate the ingredients. If the mixture is dry, add the remaining beer. If it is too moist, add more meat or bread crumbs.

3. Shape the mixture into 6 patties and set aside on a plate.

4. In a large skillet, melt the butter over medium-high heat. Arrange the patties in the skillet, reduce the heat to medium, and cook until the patties are nicely browned, about 10 minutes total. Use a spatula to gently turn the patties and it is better to let the first side cook longer, as the patties tend to crumble if they are not thoroughly cooked. Remove the skillet from the heat when done.

5. Lightly toast the bread slices, then spread each with tartar sauce. Make the sandwiches by placing a patty, along with a slice of tomato, onion, and lettuce between two pieces of toasted bread. Serve immediately.

"Spice a dish with love and it pleases every palate."
—*Titus Maccius Plautus*

Soups & Stews

You wouldn't think that soups and stews have anything to do with theories of evolution, but there may be more to the story than you realize!

The dictionary defines the word primogenitor as a first parent or earliest ancestor. It follows with the definition of primordial as constituting a beginning, or pertaining to—or existing from—the very beginning.

From these scientific definitions, modern scientists, of the school believing that all life developed and emerged from the sea, have nicknamed sea water as primordial soup. And Shoalwater Kitchen certainly proved this point, adding primordial stews to the menu because delicious liquid oyster recipes become a part of you when they are consumed.

Quiet, Please!
The Oyster dwells beneath the waves
Where all is calm and quiet;
He only opens his shelly jaws
To get his daily diet.

He abhors a curse, and what is worse.
To him a noise and clamor;
He defends his life against your knife
In a tight, jaw clamping manner.

Now, openers, harken to my plea,
If your job's to bring you joy, sir;
Be calm and still as you pry his "bill."
For a noise annoys an Oyster.

—*The Sou'wester (Summer 1968, Vol. III, No. 2)*
The Pacific County Historical Society
State of Washington

Oyster Stew

This basic recipe includes a list of various ways to embellish, improve, change, create, and glorify this famous dish. No matter how you make your stew, be sure you do not boil the milk, do not overcook the oysters, and do serve the finished masterpiece in heated bowls. Have oyster crackers readily at hand, and offer dill pickles for a traditional zesty accent. For a hearty supper, serve fresh homemade baked bread or warmed sourdough bread, and follow the meal with deep-dish apple pie.

Serves 4

1 pint shucked oysters (preferably small)
6 tablespoons (3/4 stick) butter
1 quart milk or half-and-half
Salt
Freshly ground black pepper
Dash of hot pepper sauce, such as Tabasco
Paprika or dried parsley (optional)

1. Preheat the oven to 250°F.

2. In a medium skillet over medium heat, sauté the oysters with their liquor in 2 tablespoons of butter until their edges begin to curl (do not exceed 5 minutes). Set aside.

3. Heat the milk in a large saucepan over medium-low heat and add any flavor variations at this time (see list below). Do not boil. Mix in the oysters with their liquor and simmer until heated through, 5 to 8 minutes.

Additional embellishments:

• Add 1/4 teaspoon grated nutmeg.

• Add 1/4 teaspoon grated nutmeg, 1 bay leaf, and 1 tablespoon dried parsley.

- Add 1 teaspoon tarragon or thyme.

- Sauté 1/2 cup minced onions and celery in butter, then add it to the milk and oysters.

- Add finely minced garlic and a dash of cayenne pepper.

- Add a few drops Angostura bitters.

- Add 1 tablespoon curry powder.

- Add 1 teaspoon dry mustard.

4. Season to taste with salt, black pepper, and hot pepper sauce. Add 2 tablespoons of butter and heat until it is melted.

5. Heat 4 ovenproof bowls in the warm oven.

6. Pour the oyster stew into each bowl and top with 1/2 tablespoon of butter and a sprinkling of paprika or parsley per serving. Serve hot.

Said one Oyster to another,
In a tone of pure delight,
"I'll meet you in the kitchen,
And we'll both get stewed tonight."
—Author unknown

Oyster and Spinach Soup

Marge Welling, a good friend and faithful oyster taster of many recipes in this book, came up with this absolutely delicious and heart-warming soup. Its flavor is superb and subtle, although not too rich. And because it is as attractive as it is tasty, you can serve it in soup plates instead of bowls. For those who like cold soup on hot summer evenings, serve this soup ice cold as a first course, with Melba toast and chilled white wine.

Serves 4

4 tablespoons (1/2 stick) butter
2 1/2 teaspoons minced garlic
1 pint shucked oysters (preferably small)
1 medium lemon
4 cups milk
1/3 cup all-purpose flour
1 teaspoon Dijon mustard
1/2 tablespoon fresh basil
2 bay leaves
2 cups finely chopped spinach
3 scallions, green parts only, chopped
1 teaspoon salt
Freshly ground black pepper

1. Preheat the oven to 250°F.

2. Melt the butter in a large soup pot. Add the garlic and oysters with their liquor to the pot and simmer until the oysters plump and their edges curl. Remove the pot from the heat and set aside.

3. Cut 6 paper-thin lemon slices—rind and all—then finely chop the thin slices and add them to the pot with the oysters.

4. In a small bowl, combine 1 cup of milk and the flour, blending until smooth. Mix in the mustard and set aside.

5. Heat 4 ovenproof soup bowls or soup plates in the warm oven.

6. Add to the soup the basil, bay leaves, mustard mixture, remaining milk, spinach, scallions, salt, and the black pepper, to taste. Cook over low heat until heated through, about 20 minutes; do not boil. Serve hot in warmed soup bowls.

TIP: To skin garlic, lightly smash it with the flat side of a knife. The skin will split for easy removal.

Did you know?

Casanova ate fifty (oysters) every evening with his punch, so he says, as a man in his fix nowadays, faced with the grind of perpetual romance, would probably take pep drugs, but others did as much out of nothing but a healthy appetite and enjoyment of their food.

—The Oysters of Locmariaquer, 1964
Eleanor Clark

Tomato Shoop

Perfect for fair and foul weather alike, serve this shoop with the Oyster-Hamburger Sandwich (page 72). Though it does not contain oysters, it simply cannot go without mention when paired alongside the oyster sandwich recipes.

Serves 4

1 (16-ounce) can stewed tomatoes
1 (28-ounce) can whole tomatoes
1 medium onion, chopped
1 cup coarsely chopped celery stalks
4 tablespoons (1/2 stick) butter
4 tablespoons all-purpose flour
2 cups chicken broth
1/2 teaspoon sugar
1/8 teaspoon paprika
1/2 teaspoon chopped fresh basil
1 bay leaf
Oyster liquor (optional)
4 tablespoons Worcestershire sauce
4 ounces gin

1. In a large saucepan, cook the stewed and whole tomatoes, with their juice, the onion, and celery over medium heat until the mixture starts to boil. Stir, reduce the heat to low, and simmer for 15 minutes. Pour and mash the mixture through a fine-mesh strainer into a large bowl and set aside.

2. Melt the butter in the same saucepan over medium heat, then add the flour and blend until smooth. Add the chicken broth, sugar, paprika, basil, and bay leaf; stir and bring to a boil.

3. Add the strained tomatoes and oyster liquor, if using, and simmer for 30 minutes, uncovered.

4. In individual soup bowls, place 1 tablespoon Worcestershire sauce and 1 ounce gin. Fill each with the steaming soup and serve hot.

Clear Oyster Soup

*This light and subtle soup was the first place award winner at the 1984
Washington State Seafood Competition. It makes an excellent first
course, similar to the clear and flavorful soups served in Japan.
Sake or a light, dry white wine is the perfect accompaniment.*

Serves 6

1/2 cup (1 stick) butter
1 cup finely chopped celery
1 cup finely chopped scallions, plus more (sliced into 1-inch pieces),
   to serve
1/4 cup finely chopped red bell pepper
1 tablespoon all-purpose flour
1 teaspoon minced garlic
2 bay leaves
3 slices lemon, finely chopped (rind included)
1 quart shucked or jarred oysters, liquor reserved
1/4 cup white wine
1/2 teaspoon salt
Freshly ground black pepper

1. In a medium skillet, melt the butter over medium heat. Add the
   celery, scallions, and bell pepper. Cook until tender.

2. Add the flour to the skillet and cook over low heat, stirring,
   for 5 minutes.

3. Mix in the garlic, bay leaves, and lemon and simmer for 20 minutes.

4. In a medium bowl, add enough water to the reserved oyster liquor to
   make 6 cups.

5. Combine the oyster liquor and water with the wine in a large soup pot. Add the vegetable-flour mixture and oysters to the pot. Simmer over medium-low heat for 20 minutes or until the oysters float and their edges curl.

6. Add the salt and the black pepper, to taste, then remove the bay leaves.

7. For each serving, place 4 oysters with the hot broth in a warm soup plate. Garnish with the scallion pieces and serve.

Did you know?

The poet Ausonius, during the fourth century, speaks of oysters with the same enthusiasm as Montaigne, who visited France, the Bordeaux region, on a parliamentary mission in 1581. "They brought us oysters in baskets," Montaigne wrote, describing a shore dinner in the neighborhood. "They are so agreeable, and of so high an ardor of taste, that it is like smelling violets to eat them; moreover they are so healthy, a valet gobbled up more than a hundred without any disturbance." And in another passage: "To be subject to the colic, and to be deprived of oysters, is two evils for one; since we have to choose between the two, we might as well risk something in the pursuit of pleasure."

*—The Oysters of Locmariaquer, 1964
Eleanor Clark*

About Gumbo

Enter a traditional Creole restaurant in New Orleans and you're sure to find gumbo on the menu. This thick dish, similar to stew, is always served over rice and combines many types of vegetables, shellfish, sausage, and fowl. Oysters, however, added at the last minute to any combination, truly add a flavor not obtained by any other ingredient.

There are a few important ingredients and steps that make gumbos a total success. Filé powder, made from sassafras and thyme leaves, is one of the main ingredients. Originally discovered by the Choctaw Indians, it is highly seasoned and used as a thickening agent. It should be added at the last minute and should not be reheated, as it loses its thickening powers and may become stringy. Fresh or frozen okra can be substituted when filé powder is unavailable or when both are desired in the recipe. Just cut the filé powder amount in half.

The roux is another key element, creating the smoky flavor in gumbo. It is simply butter, oil, and flour slowly simmered over low heat for 20 to 30 minutes until a rich golden brown color has been obtained.

For a slight change to any gumbo, add chicken pieces to the soup pot. Cut up a stewing chicken, using the breasts, thighs, legs, and wings for the gumbo and the remaining parts for the broth. Just brown the chicken pieces lightly before adding them along with the broth to the gumbo.

Oyster and Sausage Gumbo

A good friend and excellent chef, Steve Billy, first introduced me to this simply delicious combination of flavors. Though this recipe isn't exactly like his, it is a very tasty contender. Serve with a tossed green salad, drizzled with Caesar dressing, warm French bread or sourdough rolls, and a hearty red wine.

Note: Be sure to read "About Gumbos" on page 87 for additional information.

Serves 6 to 8

Roux:
6 tablespoons (3/4 stick) butter
1/4 cup vegetable oil
1/2 cup all-purpose flour

Base:
2 cups chopped onion
2/3 cup chopped green bell pepper
3 scallions, chopped
2 tablespoons minced garlic
2 quarts fresh or canned chicken broth
1/2 pound baked ham, cubed
1 pound spicy smoked sausage, sliced (preferably andouille)
2 tablespoons chopped fresh parsley
1 quart shucked oysters
Hot cooked rice, to serve

Spices:
1 teaspoon freshly ground black pepper
1/8 teaspoon cayenne pepper
1 teaspoon dried thyme
2 bay leaves, crushed

1/8 teaspoon dried mace or ground nutmeg
1 tablespoon salt
2 tablespoons filé powder or 1 pound fresh or frozen okra (stems
  removed and sliced into 1/2-inch pieces)

  * *Special Note: If using both filé powder and okra, cut the amount of filé
    powder in half.*

1. To prepare the roux, melt the butter in a 6- to 8-quart soup pot over
   medium heat. Add the vegetable oil and reduce the heat to low. Cook
   for 2 minutes, gradually adding the flour, 1 tablespoon at a time, and
   thoroughly blending with the butter and oil after each addition. When
   all the flour is added, continue to simmer, stirring until the roux is
   golden brown and has a smoky aroma. Be sure the heat is low; if the
   heat is too high, you will burn the flour. Simmer for approximately 25
   minutes, stirring occasionally to keep the mixture blended. Your result
   should be the color of hazelnuts—a rich golden brown.

(continued on next page)

2. Start adding the base ingredients to the roux in the soup pot. Add the onion, bell pepper, scallions, and garlic. Stir thoroughly, then mix in 1/4 cup of the chicken broth. Cook for 1 minute and add the ham, sausage, and parsley. Cook, stirring, for 15 minutes over low heat.

3. Begin adding the spices to the soup pot, starting with the black pepper, cayenne pepper, thyme, bay leaves, and mace. If you are using fresh chicken broth, mix in the salt. If you are using canned broth, taste before adding any salt, as canned broth usually has salt added already. Stir thoroughly.

4. Pour the remaining chicken broth into the pot. Increase the heat to medium-high, bringing the gumbo to a slight boil. Immediately reduce the heat to low and simmer uncovered for 1 1/2 hours, stirring occasionally to prevent sticking. If okra is being used, add it at this time.

5. Drain the oysters and add their liquor to the gumbo. Set the oysters aside.

6. Check the broth in the soup pot, taste for seasoning, and adjust accordingly. Add the oysters and cook about 5 minutes, until their edges begin to curl.

7. Remove the pot from the heat and add the filé powder. Stir thoroughly and let stand for 5 minutes. Do not reheat after the filé powder is added. Serve the gumbo over the hot cooked rice, giving each person plenty of oysters, sausage, and a healthy serving of the rich sauce.

TIP: The gumbo may be prepared through step 5 ahead of time and then chilled until it is ready to be used. Just reheat 15 minutes before completing the recipe as directed and serve.

Did you know?

An oyster eats, as it breathes, by pumping water in and out of its valves more or less continually, at a rate that is awesome. At the most favorable temperature, said to be 77°F for at least some species, they take through themselves from 1 to 6 liters an hour. At this rate, an average sized human would take in the contents of sixty-two full bathtubs every hour, or in twenty-four hours would work through a large public swimming pool. In the case of the oyster, the pumping mechanism for this vast operation is nothing but a lot of little lashes, or cilia, lining the pleats of its breathing apparatus, or branchiate; said lashes being in a frantic state of motion that creates a current whereby the seawater and the particles of nourishment in it go roaring through the valves. As it takes at least a million oysters to make a healthy natural bank, and each one is picking out whatever it can eat before expelling the water, it all adds up to quite a commotion and quite a job of filtering. To be strictly truthful, since the microscope magnifies distance but not time, the process only looks all that frenetic. It seems calm enough to the oysters themselves.

—The Oysters of Locmariaquer, *1964*
Eleanor Clark

Main Courses

At first glance, some of the recipes in this section may seem to be a tad complicated or involved. Really, they are designed for all categories of cooks. If you read the directions thoroughly before beginning and have all your ingredients and equipment at hand, you will have a lot of fun creating an outstanding meal. Pacific oysters can be very large and are recommended for all recipes that call for chopped oysters.

Scalloped Oysters

When confronted with that person who says, "No, thank you," whenever oysters are offered, this is the dish to serve! Layered with seasoned oysters and buttery crackers, very few can resist it. The New England purist would use saltines or pilot crackers, but Ritz crackers can also be used. They are richer, and their color adds to the attractiveness of the dish. Serve at a buffet, a potluck, or any time you're in the mood for oysters!

Serves 4

1 quart shucked oysters
1/2 cup (1 stick) butter, melted
1/2 pint heavy cream
3 cups coarsely broken crackers
Several dashes of nutmeg
1/2 teaspoon freshly ground black pepper
Salt
Butter

1. Preheat the oven to 400°F.

2. Drain the oysters, reserving the liquor. Set both aside.

3. Melt the butter in a medium saucepan over medium heat. Remove from heat and mix in the reserved oyster liquor and heavy cream. Set aside.

4. Grease a 7 x 7-inch casserole dish and line the bottom with 1 cup of crushed crackers. Arrange a layer of oysters over the crackers, drizzle one-third of the cream sauce over the oysters, and sprinkle lightly with the nutmeg, pepper, and salt, to taste. Repeat with another layering of crackers, oysters, cream sauce, and seasonings. Top with the remaining crushed crackers, then drizzle the remaining cream sauce over all. Dot with butter.

5. Bake for 20 minutes, until the casserole is golden brown and sizzling. Serve hot.

Shoalwater Beer–Steamed Oysters

Years ago, while on vacation and walking around the port and quaint side streets of Key West, Florida, my husband and I came upon a small outdoor seafood restaurant. The palm trees were swaying in the soft tropical breeze, which carried the intriguing aroma of shrimp steamed in beer. We suggested that the cook steam oysters similarly, and the result was unforgettable. As we left, we were asked to sign one of our dollar bills, as we were the very first customers of this brand new little restaurant. Here is the recipe from that memorable day, and it has proven to be equally delicious eaten under Pacific Northwest pine trees.

Serves 4

2 (12-ounce) bottles or cans beer (preferably dark ale—one for the pot and one for the cook!)
1 bay leaf
4 whole cloves
10 whole black peppercorns
24 medium oysters, in their shells, or more as needed (allow at least 6 per person)
Shoalwater Tartar Sauce, to serve (page 149; optional)
Shoalwater Cocktail Sauce, to serve (page 151; optional)
Hot Garlic Butter Sauce, to serve (page 156)
Soy-Mirin Sauce, to serve (page 157; optional)

1. Pour 1 can of beer into a large soup pot, then add the bay leaf, cloves, and whole peppercorns. Cook over medium heat for 10 minutes to meld the flavors. Turn heat off.

2. Scrub the oysters and place them into the pot with the deep side of the shells down.

3. Cover the pot and turn the heat on to high. Steam until the oysters begin to open, 5 to 8 minutes. Watch carefully as beer will foam up. Turn off heat and let rest for 5 minutes.

4. With tongs, carefully remove the oysters from the pot.

5. Open the oysters with an oyster knife or supply your guests with oyster knives and towels. Serve with a choice of tartar sauce, cocktail sauce, garlic butter sauce, and/or soy-mirin sauce for dipping.

Did you know?

As many as 200,000 bushels of oysters were shipped annually to California between 1850 and 1900.

Oyster-Mushroom Casserole

*This creamy casserole is easily made by a beginning cook; just make sure
to read through all the instructions before proceeding. Sweet pickled
watermelon rind provides a tart accent, and a dry white wine is also
fitting for this splendid entrée.*

Serves 6

1 quart shucked oysters
1/2 pound mushrooms
6 tablespoons (3/4 stick) butter
1 medium green bell pepper, seeded and finely chopped
4 scallions, chopped
2 cups half-and-half
2 tablespoons all-purpose flour
Dash of ground nutmeg
Dash of paprika
Dash of cayenne pepper
1 cup freshly grated Parmesan cheese
1/4 cup Madeira wine or dry sherry
Freshly ground black pepper
Salt
1/4 cup dry fine bread crumbs
Hot cooked brown and white rice (mixed), to serve

1. Preheat the oven to 450°F and grease a 9 x 11-inch baking dish.

2. Drain the oysters, reserving the liquor. Set both aside.

3. Wash the mushrooms and wipe clean with a cloth. Remove and chop
   the stems, leaving the caps whole. Set aside.

4. Melt 4 tablespoons of butter in a large skillet over medium heat. Add the bell pepper, scallions, and chopped mushroom stems and sauté until soft, approximately 3 minutes. Mix in the whole mushroom caps, coating well with butter, and cook for 1 to 2 minutes. Remove the skillet from the heat and set aside.

5. Heat the half-and-half in a small saucepan over low heat; do not boil.

6. In the meantime, melt the remaining butter in the top of a double boiler over medium heat. Add the flour, whisk until smooth, then cook for 3 more minutes.

7. Slowly add the heated half-and-half to the double boiler, stirring constantly, until thickened. Stir in the nutmeg, paprika, cayenne pepper, 2 tablespoons of Parmesan cheese, and the Madeira wine; whisk until smooth. Taste for seasoning and add black pepper and salt as desired. Remove from heat and set aside.

8. In a small bowl, mix 1/4 cup of Parmesan cheese with the bread crumbs and set aside. Pour the remaining cheese in a shallow dish.

9. Roll each oyster in the dish of Parmesan cheese, then arrange the oysters in a single layer in the baking dish. Spread the vegetable mixture evenly over the top and pour the cream sauce over the entire dish. Sprinkle with the cheese-bread crumb mixture.

10. Bake until the oysters are plump and the casserole starts to bubble, approximately 8 minutes.

11. Spoon the casserole over servings of cooked rice and serve hot.

Spanish Chicken–Oyster Casserole

This is Shoalwater Kitchen's variation on Jambalaya, using local shellfish. You may add steamer clams or large shrimp. Thinly sliced squid in place of the razor clams is also a nice variation. This flavorful dish is best served with a crisp green salad (topped by avocado or garbanzo beans) and a side dish of small cooked red beans. A bottle of Burgundy or Pinot Noir adds just the right finish to this delightful spread. Salud!

Serves 6

Broth:
1 (3 to 4-pound) chicken
1 medium onion
2 whole cloves
Crushed black peppercorns
2 bay leaves
1 medium celery stalk
2 medium carrots

Casserole:
1 pint shucked oysters, or more if desired
All-purpose flour
Freshly ground black pepper
Salt
7 tablespoons olive oil
5 tablespoons butter
1 large onion, chopped
1/2 medium green bell pepper, seeded and sliced into thin slivers
1/2 cup chopped celery
Pinch of cayenne pepper
Pinch of saffron threads
1 tablespoon dried oregano

1 1/2 teaspoons dried basil
1/2 teaspoon dried thyme
1 teaspoon cumin
1/2 teaspoon sugar
1 (4-ounce) jar pimentos, drained
1 teaspoon minced garlic
1 1/2 cups rice
1/2 cup 1-inch vermicelli pieces
1 (28-ounce) can diced tomatoes
1/4 cup red wine
1 cup pitted black olives, sliced
1 cup frozen green peas, thawed
1 cup diced razor clams, whole steamed clams, or whole squid

1. To make the broth, cut up the chicken: halve the breasts and remove the thighs, legs, and wings. Set aside, reserving the remaining pieces—including the bones.

2. Cover the remaining chicken pieces and bones with water in a large soup pot. Boil and cook for a few minutes, skimming off the scum that rises to the top. Stud the onion with the cloves and add it to the pot with peppercorns, to taste, the bay leaves, celery, and carrots. Simmer for approximately 1 hour over medium-low heat.

3. While the broth is cooking, begin making the rest of the casserole. Drain the oysters and reserve their liquor. Set both aside.

4. In a shallow dish, season the flour with black pepper and salt. Dip in the chicken breasts, legs, and thighs and lightly coat, adding more seasoned flour as needed.

(continued on next page)

5. Lightly brown the coated chicken pieces in 5 tablespoons of olive oil and 3 tablespoons of butter in a large skillet over medium-high heat. The breasts will cook faster, so remove them promptly when lightly browned and transfer them to a platter. Brown the remaining pieces about 3 minutes longer; total browning time should not exceed 5 minutes. (The browning is done to achieve a crisp coating, not to cook the chicken.) Transfer all the pieces to the platter and set aside.

6. Drain off the excess fat in the skillet, leaving approximately 2 to 3 tablespoons for sautéing. Add the onion, bell pepper, and celery to the skillet. Sauté over medium heat until soft, about 7 minutes. Add the cayenne pepper, saffron, oregano, basil, thyme, cumin, and salt and black pepper, to taste. Follow with the sugar, pimentos, and garlic, stir, and remove from heat.

7. Preheat the oven to 350°F.

8. In a deep roasting pan, melt the remaining butter and olive oil over medium heat. Add the rice and vermicelli and sauté until light brown, about 5 minutes. This adds a nut-like flavor. Add the tomatoes with their juice, the sautéed vegetables, reserved oyster liquor, the wine, olives, peas, and clams. Adjust the seasonings as desired and mix thoroughly.

9. The chicken broth should be cooked by this time. Pour it through a strainer, taste and adjust the seasonings, then add approximately 4 cups to the roasting pan, or enough to cover and cook the rice.

10. Arrange the browned chicken pieces on top of the casserole, cover the roaster with aluminum foil, and bake for 30 minutes.

11. Remove the foil, arrange the oysters on top of the chicken, and replace the foil. Bake for an additional 15 minutes or until the rice is cooked and the liquid has been absorbed.

12. To serve, put a scoop of hot rice on each plate and top with a chicken piece and a few oysters.

Oyster Supper

Do not be discouraged by the length of this recipe; it is really quite simple to prepare. Topped with homemade biscuits resting on a creamy cheese center of oysters and vegetables, it makes an excellent main course for a buffet or large party. Serve with a dry white wine to complement the flavors.

Serves 6

Biscuits:
2 cups all-purpose flour
2 teaspoons baking powder
1 teaspoon salt
5 tablespoons butter
3/4 cup milk

Cream sauce:
4 tablespoons (1/2 stick) butter
4 tablespoons all-purpose flour
1 1/2 cups heavy cream
1 cup milk
1/2 cup freshly grated Parmesan cheese
Salt and pepper
Dash of cayenne pepper
Dash of ground nutmeg

Oyster–vegetable filling:
1 pint shucked oysters
3 tablespoons butter
1 small green bell pepper, seeded and coarsely chopped
1 medium onion, coarsely chopped
1/4 pound mushrooms, sliced
1/2 cup pimentos
1 pound bacon, sliced (optional)

1. To make the biscuits, sift the flour, baking powder, and salt into a medium bowl. Cut in the butter with a pastry blender or 2 knives

until the mixture is crumbly. Add the milk and lightly knead with your hands to form a ball.

2. Turn the dough out onto a lightly floured surface and knead for 30 seconds. Roll to a 1/2 inch thickness and cut into rounds with a biscuit cutter. Set aside.

3. To make the cream sauce, melt the butter in the top of a double boiler over medium heat. Add the flour, blend, and cook for 2 minutes. Slowly add the cream and cook until thickened. Then pour in the milk in a slow, thin stream and stir.

4. Add the Parmesan cheese, salt and pepper, to taste, cayenne pepper, and nutmeg to the double boiler. Cook, stirring until thick, about 5 minutes. Set aside.

5. Preheat the oven to 425°F.

6. To make the filling, cook the oysters in their liquor in a medium skillet over medium heat until their edges curl, about 5 to 8 minutes. Drain, cool, and coarsely chop; set aside.

7. In a medium skillet over medium heat, melt the butter. Add the bell pepper and onion and cook until soft, about 5 minutes. Mix in the mushrooms, pimentos, and chopped oysters and cook for 2 more minutes. Set aside.

8. If using, cook the bacon in a large skillet over medium-high heat until crisp, about 10 to 15 minutes. Drain on paper towels and crumble when cool. Set aside.

9. Combine the cream sauce and oyster-vegetable mixture in a large bowl and pour into a shallow, 9 x 11-inch casserole dish. Sprinkle with the crumbled bacon, if using, and top with a single layer of biscuits. Bake any extra biscuits separately.

10. Bake the casserole about 12 minutes, until the biscuits are browned. Serve hot.

Oyster-Spinach Soufflé

The secret to making a successful soufflé is to gently fold in the egg whites when blending them into the filling. All hands should be at the table when the soufflé is brought in; if the soufflé is left to cool, it will fall. Although it is still edible, the soufflé loses its signature presentation. Serve alongside a whole baked fish for a truly impressive meal.

Serves 4

1 (10-ounce) package frozen chopped spinach
2 scallions, chopped
1 pint shucked oysters
3 tablespoons butter
3 tablespoons all-purpose flour
1 cup heated milk
2 tablespoons freshly grated Parmesan cheese
5 large eggs, separated
Salt
Freshly ground black pepper
Pinch of cayenne pepper
1/8 teaspoon nutmeg

1. Preheat the oven to 375°F. Grease a 2-quart soufflé dish or straight-sided baking dish.

2. Unwrap the spinach and place it in a small saucepan over low heat. This will thaw the spinach, slowly removing excess moisture. Stir occasionally. When thawed, mix in the scallions and watch that the mixture does not burn. Drain all excess water and set aside.

3. In another small saucepan, poach the oysters in their liquor until their edges curl. Drain, cool, coarsely chop, and set aside.

4. Melt the butter in the top of a double boiler over medium heat. Blend in the flour and cook for 3 minutes. Slowly add the heated milk, stirring often to blend. Reduce the heat to low and cook until thick, about 10 minutes. Add the Parmesan cheese, stir, and set aside to cool.

5. When the white sauce is thoroughly cool, add 4 egg yolks, one at a time, beating well after each addition. Add salt and black pepper, to taste, and the cayenne pepper and nutmeg.

6. Combine the spinach, oysters, and white sauce in a large bowl; set aside.

7. In a medium bowl, beat the 5 egg whites until stiff but not dry.

8. Gently add one-quarter of the beaten egg whites to the oyster-spinach mixture and carefully blend with a wooden spoon. Add the remaining egg whites and continue to gently but thoroughly fold them in. Do not overmix!

9. Pour the mixture into the soufflé dish and bake for 30 to 40 minutes, until the top is lightly browned. Serve immediately.

Say the firm Roman to great Egypt sends
this treasure of an Oyster.
Antony and Cleopatra, 1623
—William Shakespeare

Oyster-Stuffed Bell Pepper

A variation on traditional stuffed peppers, this dish uses oysters instead of beef in its seasoned rice stuffing. Top the peppers with melted cheese, and you have an excellent-looking—and tasting—luncheon or light supper. Allow at least 1 pepper per person.

Serves 4

4 large bell peppers (color optional)
1 1/2 to 2 cups shucked oysters, fresh or canned
1 medium onion, chopped
1/4 cup olive oil
1 teaspoon dried basil
1 teaspoon dried oregano
Dash of dried marjoram
Dash of cayenne pepper
1/8 teaspoon freshly ground black pepper
1 teaspoon minced garlic
Salt
2 cups cooked rice
1 cup tomato juice, tomato sauce, or broth of choice (chicken, vegetable, etc.)
Shredded cheese of choice (optional)

1. Preheat the oven to 350°F.

2. Slice the stem end off the peppers and remove the seeds and inner membrane. Set aside.

3. Drain the oysters, discarding the liquor. Coarsely chop and set aside.

4. In a medium skillet, sauté the onions in the oil until soft, about 5 minutes. Add the basil, oregano, marjoram, cayenne pepper, black pepper, garlic, salt, to taste, and cooked rice. Cook for a few more minutes, then add the chopped oysters. Continue to cook until heated through and thoroughly blended, about 5 minutes.

5. Fill each bell pepper with the rice mixture and spoon 1 tablespoon tomato juice into each. Place the peppers in a casserole dish large enough to hold them in a single layer and surround the peppers with the remaining tomato juice.

6. Bake for 30 minutes, until the peppers are tender and the filling is hot. If using the shredded cheese, sprinkle over the tops of the peppers 10 minutes before they are done. Remove from the oven once the cheese is melted.

7. Spoon hot tomato juice around each pepper on individual plates, and serve.

Oysters Florentine

This casserole of spinach and plump oysters is always a treat. Serve it with rice and broiled tomatoes, and pour everybody a nice glass of chilled, dry white wine. A variation with mushrooms follows.

Serves 6

Cream sauce:
2 cups half-and-half
2 tablespoons butter
2 tablespoons all-purpose flour
Dash of ground nutmeg
Dash of paprika
Dash of cayenne pepper
Salt and pepper
2 tablespoons freshly grated Parmesan cheese
1 tablespoon freshly squeezed lemon juice
1/4 cup Madeira wine or dry sherry

Spinach-oyster filling:
2 pounds spinach, washed and trimmed, or 2 (1-pound) packages
    frozen spinach
2 tablespoons butter
3/4 cup finely chopped green bell pepper
3 scallions, chopped
1 quart shucked oysters
1 1/2 cups freshly grated Parmesan cheese
1/2 cup fine dry bread crumbs

1. To make the cream sauce, heat the half-and-half in a small saucepan over medium heat; do not boil. Remove from the heat and set aside.

2. In the top of a double boiler, melt the butter over medium heat. Add the flour and whisk until smooth. Cook a few more minutes, stirring constantly. Slowly add the heated half-and-half, continuously stirring

until thick and smooth. Stir in the nutmeg, paprika, cayenne pepper, and salt and pepper, to taste. Add the Parmesan cheese, lemon juice, and Madeira wine and stir until blended. Set aside.

3. Make the spinach-oyster filling. If using fresh spinach, steam in a medium saucepan over boiling water until wilted. Drain and chop. If using frozen spinach, thaw, squeeze out the excess liquid, and chop. Set aside.

4. In a medium saucepan over medium heat, melt the butter. Add the bell pepper and scallions and cook until soft, about 7 minutes. Stir in the spinach and cook a few more minutes.

5. Combine the spinach mixture with the cream sauce in a medium bowl. Blend and set aside.

6. Preheat the oven to 450°F.

7. Spread the creamed spinach over the bottom of a 9 x 11-inch baking dish. Set aside.

8. Drain the oysters, discarding the liquor or reserving for another use. Roll each oyster in a shallow bowl filled with the Parmesan cheese.

9. Arrange the oysters in a single layer on top of the spinach in the casserole. Mix the leftover cheese with the bread crumbs and sprinkle on top of the casserole.

10. Bake for approximately 8 minutes or until the casserole starts to bubble and the oysters are plump.

11. In order to include all the layers, use a wide spatula when dishing up the casserole. Serve hot.

Oysters Florentine with Mushrooms: Prepare Oysters Florentine through step 8. Sauté sliced fresh mushrooms and add them to the creamed spinach. Complete the recipe as directed.

Scalloped Potato and Oyster Casserole

This fine casserole is not only a main course, but also makes a marvelous accompaniment for steak or baked ham. Layered with potatoes and oysters, the cracker–cheese topping is a delicious introduction to the goodies that lie beneath it.

Serves 4

4 large potatoes
1 pint shucked oysters, fresh or jarred (preferably extra small)
1 medium onion, finely chopped
2 tablespoons chopped fresh parsley
Celery salt
Garlic powder
Salt
Freshly ground black pepper
2 tablespoons butter
Milk
1 cup shredded Cheddar cheese (about 4 ounces)
1/2 cup fine cracker crumbs

1. In a large saucepan, boil the potatoes in their skins for approximately 25 minutes. Do not overcook or the potatoes will be mushy. Drain and rinse in cold water. The potatoes will be easier to handle if cooked and chilled ahead of time. Peel and cut into thin slices; set aside.

2. If using fresh oysters, cook over low heat in a medium saucepan with their liquor until their edges begin to curl, about 5 to 8 minutes. Drain and reserve the liquor. If using canned oysters, drain and reserve the liquor. Set both aside.

3. Preheat the oven to 350°F.

4. In a deep, 2-quart casserole dish, make a layer of one-third of the potatoes, one-third of the onions, and one-third of the parsley. Sprinkle with celery salt, garlic powder, salt, and black pepper, to taste. Break up 1 tablespoon of butter into bits and dot the top. Add a layer of oysters (approximately 10). Follow with another layer of potatoes, onions, parsley, spices, butter, and oysters. Top with a final layer of potatoes and seasonings.

5. In a 2-cup glass measuring cup, add enough milk to the reserved oyster liquor to make 2 cups. Pour onto the casserole; the liquid should fill the dish about three-fourths full.

6. In a small bowl, mix the Cheddar cheese with the cracker crumbs and sprinkle evenly over the casserole.

7. Cover the dish with aluminum foil and bake for 30 minutes. Remove the foil and bake for an additional 5 minutes, until browned and a crust forms on top. Serve hot.

Did you know?

Contrary to rumor, it is perfectly safe to eat oysters at any time of the year. However, they are at their peak of goodness during the winter and spring months. During the months without an "r" (May, June, July, August), the stress of procreation makes them rather thin and watery.

Oysters and Onions

Skip this page unless you are a faithful onion lover and a true oyster lover. If you are both of the above, and are sure of your dining companions, proceed with haste and continue to sow your wild oats.

Serves 4

3 small or 2 large onions
1 pint shucked oysters
2 tablespoons butter
1 tablespoon bacon fat or oil
Salt and pepper
Toast, to serve

1. Coarsely chop the onions and set aside.

2. Drain the oysters, reserving their liquor. Set aside.

3. In a large skillet, melt 1 tablespoon of butter and the bacon fat over medium heat. Add the onions to the skillet bottom in an even layer. Add 1 cup of the reserved oyster liquor and simmer the onions until transparent, about 5 minutes.

4. Add salt and pepper, to taste, and the remaining butter. When melted, layer the oysters over the layer of onions. Cook for 5 minutes, cover, and continue cooking until the oyster edges curl, about 5 to 8 minutes.

5. Place the toast on individual plates and use a pancake turner to gently place the onion-oyster mixture on top, being careful not to disturb the layers. Serve immediately.

Oysters St. Helens

Inspired by formidable and powerful Mt. St. Helens, this dish recreates the natural phenomenon through overflowing puff pastries of piping hot oyster–cream sauce. Peas are always a nice accompaniment, but asparagus would be more appropriate in resembling downed trees. Serve pickled peppers on the side to contribute to the sensation of heat.

Serves 6

Volcanoes (puff pastry):
1 (10-ounce) package frozen puff pastry shells (6 shells)

Lava (cream sauce):
4 tablespoons (1/2 stick) butter
4 tablespoons all-purpose flour
1 1/2 cups heavy cream
1 cup milk
1/2 cup sherry
Dash of cayenne pepper
Dash of ground nutmeg
Salt and pepper

Debris (filling):
1 pint shucked oysters (earth)
3 tablespoons butter
1 medium onion, coarsely chopped (rocks)
1 small green bell pepper, seeded and coarsely chopped (foliage)
1 cup sliced mushrooms (tree stumps)
1/2 cup pimento strips (glowing coals)
Freshly ground black pepper (ash)
Paprika for garnish

1. Prepare the volcanoes according to the package directions. These can also be baked ahead of time. Remove the top from each shell and set aside to cool.

2. To make the lava, melt the butter in the top of a double boiler over medium heat. Blend in the flour and cook for 2 minutes. Slowly add the heavy cream and cook until thickened. Add the milk slowly in a thin stream, then follow with the sherry, cayenne pepper, nutmeg, and salt and pepper, to taste. Cook until thick, stirring often. Set aside.

3. Proceed with making the filling by placing the oysters with their liquor in a medium skillet and cooking them over medium heat until their edges curl, about 5 to 8 minutes. Drain, cool, and coarsely chop. Set aside.

4. In a separate medium skillet, melt the butter over medium heat. Add the onion and bell pepper and cook until soft, about 5 minutes. Mix in the mushrooms and chopped oysters and cook for 2 more minutes. Add the pimentos and black pepper, to taste, and stir to incorporate.

5. Combine the debris (oyster-vegetable mixture) with the lava sauce and keep warm.

6. On individual plates, fill each volcano to overflowing with the lava mixture, garnish with paprika, and serve steaming hot with a vegetable on the side.

Beef in Oyster Sauce

*Enjoy a taste of China with this flavorful stir-fry. For an authentic
Chinese meal, add a combination of any or all of the following:
water chestnuts, green beans, bean sprouts, pea pods, bamboo
shoots, or bok choy. Make it a multi-course event by starting off
with a clear beef broth, flavored with scallions, and serve fortune
cookies and tea for a delightful ending. You can make it even more
festive by cooking the main course at the table, allowing your
guests to have fun with "back seat cooking," while you gain added
stature in their eyes—and stomachs. A variation follows.*

Serves 6

1 cup Shoalwater oyster sauce (page 149) or commercial oyster sauce
6 tablespoons soy sauce
1 teaspoon sugar
2 tablespoons rice wine (sake) or gin
4 tablespoons oil (preferably peanut)
1/2 teaspoon minced garlic
1/2 teaspoon salt (optional)
3 pounds round steak, cut into 1-inch cubes or thinly sliced
   into 1-inch strips
2 1/2 cups boiling water
6 scallions, chopped
Cooked rice, to serve

1. In a small bowl, mix the oyster sauce, soy sauce, sugar, and sake;
   set aside.

2. Heat a wok or large iron skillet over high heat until very hot. Add
   the oil and quickly spread to coat the pan. Add the garlic and salt,
   if using. (Note: Add the salt only if you are using Shoalwater oyster
   sauce. If using commercial oyster sauce, omit the salt.) Stir and add
   the beef quickly. Stir-fry by tossing the meat so it cooks on all sides.

3. When the beef is lightly browned, add the oyster sauce mixture and stir. Cover, reduce heat to medium, and cook for 5 minutes. Pour in the boiling water and cook for 30 minutes, until the liquid is cooked down and the meat is tender. Add the scallions and stir.

4. Serve hot over cooked rice.

Beef in Oyster Sauce with Mushrooms: Follow the directions for making Beef in Oyster Sauce, adding 1/2 pound sliced fresh mushrooms with the scallions at the end of step 3. Complete the recipe as directed.

Did you know?

The romantic fallacy, the pearl idea, seems to have come in with the great voyages to the Orient, where the mollusk that came to be called the Pearl Oyster lives. The true name of the creature is Meleagrina Margaritifera. It is of the family Aviculidae and is related to the mussel, not the true oyster. For one thing, it lies on its right side. It is true that any bivalve, if annoyed by the intrusion of a grain of sand, a worm larva, or other inconvenience, may build up around it an object resembling a pearl, but if made by an oyster it will not be very pretty.

—The Oysters of Locmariaquer, 1964
Eleanor Clark

Oyster Stir-Fry

This recipe is adaptable to your choice of fresh vegetables. Use your imagination, keeping in mind the lovely color and flavor combinations that vegetables create. When added to this recipe's fresh oysters, peanuts, and spices, you'll have a winning meal every time! Just prepare all the ingredients in advance so they are available to put into the wok when the moment is right.

Serves 6

2 teaspoons corn starch
1/4 cup cold water
1/4 cup soy sauce
1 1/2 tablespoons peanut oil
Minced fresh ginger or powdered ginger
1 medium onion, sliced diagonally
2 medium carrots, cut into thin 2-inch strips
2 medium celery stalks, cut diagonally into 1-inch strips
1 medium green bell pepper, seeded and cut into strips
1/2 medium zucchini, thinly sliced into rounds
1 (8-ounce) can sliced water chestnuts, drained
1 (8-ounce) can bamboo shoots, drained (optional)
1/2 teaspoon minced garlic
1 tablespoon minced fresh parsley
1/2 pound mushrooms, sliced
1 quart shucked oysters (preferably small)
1 cup fresh or canned chicken broth (preferably fresh)
1 pound fresh spinach, washed and trimmed, or 1 (10-ounce) package
    frozen leaf spinach, thawed
Cooked rice, to serve
Dry roasted peanuts, to serve
Hot sauce (optional)

1. In a small bowl, mix together the cornstarch, cold water, and soy sauce. Set aside.

2. Place the wok over high heat. When hot, add the oil and quickly spread to cover the bottom and sides. Quickly add ginger, to taste, the onions, carrots, and celery. Stir and cook for 2 minutes.

3. Add the bell pepper, zucchini, water chestnuts, and bamboo shoots, if using. Stir-fry for 1 minute. Add the garlic, parsley, and mushrooms and stir-fry for an additional minute.

4. Mix in the oysters with their liquor and gently stir, reducing the heat to medium. Continue stirring gently and cook for 1 minute.

5. Add the chicken broth and cornstarch mixture and stir. Place the spinach over all, cover, and steam for 2 minutes. Uncover and gently mix until the spinach is wilted and the liquid is thickened, about 5 minutes.

6. Serve immediately over cooked rice, topping each portion with a handful of roasted peanuts. Have a bottle of hot sauce ready for those wanting a spicier version

Did you know?

To be an oyster you have to be of course a mollusk, and a bivalvular one of the ostreid family, meaning acephalous, lamellibranchiate, monomyarian, asphonic and inequivalvular; which is to say: headless, with a crescent of tight little ruffles for breathing tubes or gills, with one muscle instead of two holding your valves together, lacking a water spout, and with one half of your shell quite different from the other. Like the other bivalves you are entirely enclosed in a sack called the mantle, a marvelous piece of material which not only fabricates every speck of shell you will ever have but also is in charge of all your sensory contact with the outside world. Unlike most other bivalves you have a peculiar habit of lying on your so-called left, that is lower or cupped, valve, heaven knows why or when the habit was acquired. However you have excellent nerves, stomach, liver, etc. and the best gills in the kingdom.

*—The Oysters of Locmariaquer, 1964
Eleanor Clark*

Shoalwater Oyster Meatballs

I recommend serving these meatballs over spaghetti, with Shoalwater Spaghetti Sauce (page 126) over the top and a sprinkling of freshly grated Parmesan cheese. Warm, crunchy garlic bread and a tossed green salad with lemon and olive oil dressing are a must with this meal. If you plan on serving plain as an hors d'oeuvre, be aware that they disappear almost instantly. Plan on making plenty!

Makes about 40

1 pint shucked oysters (preferably fresh)
1/2 pound ground beef
3/4 pound ground sausage
1/2 cup seasoned dry bread crumbs, plus more as needed
2 scallions, thinly sliced
1/2 teaspoon minced garlic
1 teaspoon dried basil
1/2 teaspoon dried oregano
1/2 teaspoon freshly ground black pepper
Salt
2 tablespoons butter
2 tablespoons olive oil
Cooked spaghetti, to serve (optional)
Hot Shoalwater Spaghetti Sauce (optional; page 126)
Freshly grated Parmesan cheese, to serve (optional)

1. Drain the oysters, reserving the liquor for another use. (Note: If you are making spaghetti sauce, add the liquor to the sauce.) Coarsely chop the oysters and set aside.

2. In a large bowl, combine the ground beef, ground sausage, bread crumbs, scallions, garlic, basil, oregano, black pepper, and salt, to taste. Mix with your hands until well blended. Add the oysters and incorporate gently by hand or with a wooden spoon.

3. Shape the beef mixture into 1-inch balls and roll them in a shallow bowl of bread crumbs. If the mixture is too soft, add more breadcrumbs as needed. Set the coated meatballs aside on a plate.

4. In a large skillet, melt the butter over medium heat. Add the olive oil, then gently add the meatballs one at a time. Do not crowd the meatballs in the pan or it will be hard to turn them. Gently shake the pan to prevent sticking. Using a spatula, gently roll the meatballs to cook them on all sides. When the meatballs are nicely browned, place them on a warm platter and keep them warm.

5. If serving as a main course with spaghetti, put the meatballs on top of hot pasta on each plate and cover with the spaghetti sauce. Sprinkle the top with Parmesan cheese and serve. (Note: If freshly grated cheese is not available, I suggest not using any at all. The pre-grated cheese in cans is of very poor quality and is not worth using.)

Shoalwater Spaghetti Sauce

Shoalwater Oyster Meatballs (page 124) are best when served with this homemade spaghetti sauce. Make the sauce ahead of time so it can simmer for at least 4 hours. The longer it simmers, the more beautifully the spices and ingredients blend together. A bottle of Cabernet Sauvignon or a robust Beaujolais served with the meal is a wonderful complement to this rich combination of flavors.

Serves 6

1 medium onion, finely chopped
1/2 medium carrot, sliced thin and chopped
1 medium celery stalk, finely chopped
Olive oil
1 (3-ounce) can tomato paste
1/4 teaspoon freshly ground black pepper
Dash of Worcestershire sauce
Pinch of cayenne pepper
1 bay leaf
1 tablespoon dried oregano
1 1/2 teaspoons minced garlic
1 tablespoon dried basil
1 teaspoon sugar
1 teaspoon salt
1 teaspoon dried thyme
2 cups beef broth, plus more as needed
1 (28-ounce) can whole tomatoes
Oyster liquor (from the oysters in Oyster Meatballs; optional)
1 1/2 cups red wine or 3/4 cup red wine and 3/4 cup port wine
1/2 pound mushrooms, sliced

1. In a large skillet, sauté the onion, carrot, and celery in 2 tablespoons of olive oil over medium heat until soft and transparent.

2. Push the vegetables to one side of the skillet. On the bare side, add the tomato paste and 1 tablespoon of olive oil and sauté for 2 minutes. (Note: This is an old trick I learned from my mother. She says it removes the sharp taste of tomato paste.)

3. Mix the skillet ingredients together and add the black pepper, Worcestershire sauce, cayenne pepper, bay leaf, oregano, garlic, basil, sugar, salt, and thyme. Cook for 2 minutes, then add the beef broth, tomatoes, and oyster liquor, if using. Reduce the heat to the lowest possible setting, stir, and simmer, uncovered, for 2 hours. Do not boil.

4. After about 2 hours, add the wine and mushrooms. If you feel more liquid is necessary, add more beef broth. Taste and correct the seasonings as needed.

5. Continue to simmer the sauce for 1 to 2 more hours. If the sauce becomes dry, add water as needed (up to 1/2 cup) to keep the right sauce consistency. Serve the sauce piping hot over cooked pasta.

Oyster Garlic Sauce Over Pasta

This recipe won first place at the Seafood Culinary Olympics in 1984 and has always been a favorite of mine. In addition to being nutritious and delicious, this meal can be prepared in only twenty minutes. Serve with crusty French bread, cucumber salad, and dry white wine.

Serves 4

1 pint shucked oysters (preferably fresh)
White wine or canned clam juice
4 tablespoons (1/2 stick) butter
1/4 cup olive oil
1/2 cup chopped scallions
1 1/2 teaspoons minced garlic
1/2 cup minced fresh parsley
1 teaspoon dried basil or 1 tablespoon minced fresh basil
1/4 teaspoon salt (optional)
1/2 teaspoon freshly ground black pepper
1 pound cooked pasta
Freshly grated Parmesan cheese, to serve

1. Drain the oysters, reserving the liquor. If there is not enough liquor to make 1 1/2 cups, add white wine or clam juice and set aside. Coarsely chop the oysters and set aside (retain all liquid).

2. In a heavy, 2-quart saucepan, melt the butter over medium heat. Add the olive oil, mix in the scallions and garlic, and cook for 2 minutes; do not let the garlic brown. (If it starts to brown, the heat is too high.) Add the parsley, basil, salt, if using, and black pepper.

3. Add the chopped oysters and the oyster liquor. Reduce the heat to low and cook about 5 minutes, until the oysters start to get plump.

4. Remove the saucepan from the heat and pour over cooked pasta in a large soup pot or casserole dish; keep warm. Let stand for a few minutes.

5. Toss to evenly distribute the sauce with the pasta before serving. Have the Parmesan cheese available at the table.

TIP: This dish can be made in advance and chilled until you are ready to use it. Just cover the casserole dish and reheat in a 350°F oven until bubbly, 15 to 20 minutes. Toss gently before serving.

Did you know?

Oysters were one of the earliest animals to be transported from one area to another and cultivated as food.

Oyster Shish Kebabs

American Indians used to lace their fish and oysters onto a stick, then drive the stick into the ground next to a fire. The stick bent over the flames and was turned to facilitate cooking. This recipe is a modern version of that method, and it makes a wonderful main course, served with rice pilaf or bulgur pilaf. As an added perk, the cooking process requires guest participation. You can also serve this recipe as an appetizer at your next cocktail party.

Serves 4

24 shucked oysters (allow 3 per skewer)
2 large tomatoes (not too ripe), cut into large chunks, or cherry tomatoes
2 medium green bell peppers, seeded and cut into large chunks
1 large onion, cut into large chunks
1/4 pound mushrooms
2 cups cubed ham
Garlic Butter Sauce (page 156)
8 wooden skewers (soaked in water for 30 minutes)

1. Prepare a fire in a gas or charcoal grill or preheat the broiler.

2. Drain the oysters and discard the liquor. Arrange the oysters attractively on a large serving platter with the tomatoes, bell pepper, onion, mushrooms, and ham.

3. In a small saucepan, make the Garlic Butter recipe.

4. Present the ingredient platter and skewers to your guests and allow them to assemble their kebabs as desired.

5. Using a pastry brush, brush the loaded skewers with garlic butter sauce before and during cooking as desired, turning the skewers frequently. If using your broiler, lay the kebabs on a baking sheet before basting.

6. Cook until you achieve the desired doneness, being careful not to overcook. Serve hot.

Broiled Oysters with Anchovy Butter

*This simple recipe is nice for a luncheon or a late-night snack.
Served on toast points and drenched in anchovy butter sauce,
these oysters are irresistible!*

Serves 4

4 tablespoons (1/2 stick) unsalted butter
4 anchovy fillets, finely chopped
1/2 teaspoon minced fresh parsley
Freshly ground black pepper
Lemon juice
1 pint shucked oysters, drained
Toast points, to serve

1. Melt the butter in a small saucepan over low heat. Stir in the anchovies, parsley, black pepper, and lemon juice, to taste. Cook for 1 minute or until blended. Set aside.

2. Preheat the broiler and grease a baking sheet.

3. Place the oysters in a single layer on the baking sheet. Broil for 2 to 3 minutes, until lightly browned. Remove from the oven.

4. Arrange the toast points on individual serving plates, place the oysters on the toast, and pour the warm anchovy butter sauce over all. Serve immediately.

*The table is a magnet which not only draws to itself
but joins together all those who approach it.*
—*L'Almanach des Gourmands, 1803*
Grimod de La Reynière

Shoalwater Creamed Oysters

ATTENTION! This is not just another creamed dish. The flavor is sublime and accompanies your favorite white wine splendidly. Serve over any number of items, from poached fish to noodles.

Serves 4

1 tablespoon butter
1 tablespoon all-purpose flour
1 cup milk, heated
12 shucked oysters, with liquor
1 teaspoon Worcestershire sauce
1 tablespoon minced fresh parsley and/or fresh tarragon
Salt
Freshly ground black pepper
Dash of cayenne pepper
Poached white fish, toast points, cooked rice, or cooked noodles, to serve

1. In a medium saucepan, melt the butter over low heat. Add the flour and blend until smooth. Slowly add the heated milk, stirring to incorporate.

2. When the sauce is thick, mix in the oysters with their liquor, the Worcestershire sauce, parsley, salt and pepper, to taste, and cayenne pepper. Continue cooking over low heat for about 10 minutes, until the oysters are plump.

3. Serve piping hot over poached white fish or other complementary food of choice.

Oyster Coquille

Ritzy in taste and appearance, this recipe features stuffed and broiled oyster shells. Serve with a green vegetable, seasoned rice, and a bottle of white wine. You can also assemble the shells hours beforehand and chill them until later. When you're ready, simply heat them in the oven until they're bubbly. This works well if you're serving them as an appetizer and need to assemble a number of dishes at once.

Serves 6

1/2 cup (1 stick) butter, softened
1/2 cup dry white wine
3/4 cup water
1 small onion, peeled and quartered
2 fresh parsley sprigs
1 bay leaf
Pinch of dried thyme
1 pint shucked oysters, with shells reserved or use ramekins
1/2 pound mushrooms, chopped
Juice of 1 medium lemon
1/2 teaspoon freshly ground black pepper
1/4 teaspoon salt
2 tablespoons all-purpose flour
4 large egg yolks
1 cup heavy cream
Bread crumbs
Freshly grated Parmesan cheese

1. In a medium saucepan over medium heat, melt 2 tablespoons of butter. Add the wine, 1/2 cup of water, the onion, parsley, bay leaf, and thyme and stir. Bring to a boil, reduce the heat to low, and simmer for 10 minutes.

2. Add the oysters to the pan and poach until the edges begin to curl. Remove with a slotted spoon, cool, chop, and set aside. Strain the broth and set aside.

3. In the same saucepan, melt 2 more tablespoons of butter over medium heat. Stir in the mushrooms, remaining water, the lemon juice, black pepper, and salt. Cook for 5 minutes, then drain, reserving the liquid and the mushrooms.

4. Add the reserved mushroom liquid and strained wine broth to the top of a double boiler, and cook over low heat.

5. Preheat the broiler.

6. Make beurre manié (page 172) with 3 tablespoons of butter and the flour. Add little pinches at a time to the double boiler, stirring after each addition. Continue to cook over low heat until smooth and thick. Stir in the chopped oysters, remove from heat, and set aside to cool.

7. In a medium bowl, beat the egg yolks with the heavy cream until thick.

8. Add the egg yolk mixture to the cooled broth in the top of the double boiler. (Note: If the broth is too hot the eggs will curdle.) Place the top pan over hot simmering water. (Note: Do not let the water boil or the egg yolks will curdle.) Cook, stirring, until the sauce is thick and smooth. Add the reserved mushrooms.

9. Place a portion of the oyster mixture into each oyster shell (the deep halves) or into individual ramekins.

10. In a small bowl, mix together some bread crumbs with the remaining butter. Sprinkle on the tops of the filled oyster shells and follow with the Parmesan cheese.

11. Place the shells under the broiler and cook until the bread crumbs are browned, about 2 to 3 minutes.

12. Serve hot in the shells, offering approximately four shells per person.

Blue Jean Hash

In the olden days of New England, the prudent housewife often made a concoction known as red flannel hash. It consisted of a variety of leftover vegetables from a boiled dinner, including corned beef. Beets were always present, thus providing the description of red. Memory of this dish came to mind when the scrumptious Shoalwater Kitchen Oyster Hash was developed, and it was immediately dubbed "Blue Jean Hash." It is really a fine combination of flavors, although there is no blue ingredient. Served with coleslaw, stewed tomatoes, and whole wheat rolls, it makes a hearty lunch or a super supper. A slice of pumpkin pie and a cup of coffee rounds out the meal—and you—in great fashion. This recipe is easily doubled if you're serving a crowd.

Serves 4

1 pint shucked oysters
2 medium potatoes
8 slices bacon
4 tablespoons (1/2 stick) butter
2 medium onions, finely chopped
Salt
Freshly ground black pepper
2 tablespoons chopped fresh parsley
1/3 cup freshly grated Parmesan cheese

1. In a small saucepan, poach fresh oysters in their own liquor. Cook over medium heat until their edges begin to curl. Remove from heat and drain, reserving the liquor for another use. Cool and chop. If using canned oysters, simply drain and chop (do not cook). Set aside.

2. In a medium saucepan, boil the potatoes in their skins for approximately 20 minutes or until done. Keep an eye on them so they do not overcook, as they will become mushy.

3. Meanwhile, cook the bacon in a large skillet over medium heat until crisp, about 10 minutes. Drain and reserve the fat. When the bacon has cooled, crumble and set aside.

4. Drain and rinse the potatoes with cold water, then peel and finely dice. Mix with the chopped oysters in a medium bowl and set aside.

5. In a large skillet over medium heat, melt the butter and add 3 tablespoons of bacon fat. Add the chopped onions and cook until transparent, about 5 minutes. Add the oyster-potato mixture to the pan and season with salt and black pepper, to taste. Mix thoroughly, then press the mixture down with a spatula.

6. Cook 10 minutes, pressing down with the spatula occasionally. This helps to form a crust on the bottom. Turn the hash in the pan, scraping up and mixing in browned parts throughout. Add the chopped parsley and press down with the spatula, cooking for 5 minutes more, or until crusty and browned.

7. Sprinkle the Parmesan cheese and crumbled bacon on top, turn the heat to low, and cover. Cook until cheese melts and serve hot.

One's stomach is one's internal environment.
—*Samuel Butler*

Oyster Hash II

Though it's hard to compete with Blue Jean Hash, this hash is a smash! Using mashed potatoes and adding the spice of ginger and the slight bite of cayenne pepper, it stands on its own. Serve with Shoalwater Cocktail Sauce (page 151) and quartered lemons for extra zing.

Serves 4

4 medium potatoes, peeled
Salt and pepper
1 pint shucked oysters
1/4 cup minced onion
1/4 cup minced fresh parsley
Ginger
Cayenne pepper
2 tablespoons butter
1 tablespoon bacon fat or oil

1. In a large saucepan over medium heat, boil the potatoes until tender, about 15 minutes. Drain, mash, and season to taste with salt and pepper. Set aside.

2. Poach the oysters in their liquor in a small saucepan over medium heat. Cool, drain, and chop coarsely, reserving the liquor for another use.

3. In a large bowl, combine the oysters with the mashed potatoes, onion, parsley, ginger, cayenne pepper, and salt and pepper, to taste. Set aside.

4. Melt the butter and bacon fat in a large skillet over medium heat. Add the potato-oyster mixture and cook for 10 minutes, until lightly browned.

5. With a spatula, gently turn the hash and press, incorporating any browned parts. Fry until golden brown and serve hot.

Shoalwater Kitchen Stuffing

This rich stuffing can be used for fish or fowl, or it can be baked by itself. Just allow 1/2 to 3/4 cup stuffing for every pound of meat. A list of simple but signature variations follows.

About 7 1/2 cups

1/2 cup (1 stick) butter
1/2 cup celery, chopped
1/2 cup onion, chopped
1 1/4 cups white wine, broth of choice, milk, or water
1 (8 1/2-ounce) can sliced water chestnuts, drained
1 pint shucked oysters, drained and chopped or left whole if small
1/2 cup minced fresh parsley
1 teaspoon dried sage
Dash of ground bay leaves or 1 bay leaf, crushed
1 teaspoon dried basil
1/2 teaspoon paprika
1/8 teaspoon ground nutmeg
1/2 teaspoon freshly ground black pepper
1/4 teaspoon dried thyme
1/2 pound sausage meat, cooked (optional)
1/4 cup brandy
5 cups toasted French bread cubes

1. Melt the butter over medium heat in a large, heavy skillet. Add the celery and onion and sauté until soft, about 5 minutes.

2. Mix in a 1/2 cup of white wine, the water chestnuts, chopped oysters, parsley, sage, bay leaves, basil, paprika, nutmeg, black pepper, and thyme. Continue cooking for a few more minutes.

3. Empty the mixture into a large bowl, add the cooked sausage, if using, the brandy, bread cubes and remaining white wine. Toss lightly to incorporate all and use as directed. If baking separately, put the stuffing in a greased loaf pan and bake in a 350°F oven for 45 minutes, until the top is browned. Serve hot.

Variations:

• Add diced green bell pepper or carrots in step 1.

• Add 2 lightly beaten eggs in step 3. This makes a heavier stuffing.

• Delete the cooked sausage meat and add 1 additional pint of oysters, draining and chopping as directed.

• Add 1 cup sliced mushrooms, or more to taste, in step 1.

• Add 1 cup nuts of choice (preferably pecans, walnuts, Brazil nuts, pine nuts, or chestnuts) in step 3.

• Substitute cooked rice for the bread cubes.

Food for Thought

According to Jean Anthelme Brillat-Savarin, who wrote the most noted literary tributes to the table and to all aspects of gastronomy, this is why food and cooking are so beloved.

Taste is a sense that, all things considered, procures us the greatest number of enjoyments:

1st. Because the pleasure of eating is the only one that, taken in moderation, is never followed by fatigue;

2nd. Because it belongs to all time, to all ages, and to all conditions;

3rd. Because it occurs necessarily at least once a day, and may be repeated without inconvenience two or three times in this space of time;

4th. Because it may be combined with all our other pleasures and even console us for their absence;

5th. Because the impressions it receives are at the same time more durable and more dependent on our will;

6th. Because in eating we receive a certain indefinable and special comfort which arises from the intuitive consciousness that we repair our losses and prolong our existence by the food we eat.

Lastly, the tongue of man, by the delicacy of its texture and the various membranes which environ it, sufficiently indicates the sublimity of the operations for which it is destined. It contains at least three movements unknown to animals, which he terms spication, rotation, and verrition. The first is when the tongue in a conical shape comes from between the lips that compress it; the second, when the tongue moves circularly in the space comprised between the interior of the cheeks and the palate; the third, when the tongue, curving upwards or downwards, gathers anything remaining in the semicircular canal formed by the lips and gums.

—*The Pleasures of the Table*, 1902
Jean Anthelme Brillat-Savarin

Sauces

There are numerous premade sauces and salad dressings available on the market, and they come in various forms—bottled, powdered, etc. It is the purpose of this chapter to enable you to create your own sauces from scratch, impressing you and your guests with the delightful play of fresh ingredients on your tastebuds. And you'll be happy to know that making fresh sauces is quite simple and often incorporates ingredients that you already have on hand. You may never go back to that pesky bottled variety again!

Shoalwater Oyster Sauce

In Chinese markets or the gourmet section of your favorite grocery store, you can find bottled, oyster-flavored sauce, but this is a far superior sauce made from fresh oysters. It is potent and can be used with other ingredients in marinades. Try a tablespoon or two in spaghetti sauces, teriyaki marinade, or other dark sauces.

Makes 1 cup

1 cup shucked oysters, fresh or canned
Canned clam juice, as needed
4 tablespoons soy sauce
1 teaspoon sugar
1 teaspoon salt
2 teaspoons molasses
1 tablespoon all-purpose flour
1 1/2 tablespoons water

1. Pour fresh oysters with their liquor in a medium saucepan. If there is not enough liquor to make 1 cup, add enough clam juice to make up the difference. Simmer over low heat for 25 minutes, then remove from the heat and cool. If using canned oysters, proceed to step 2.

2. Purée the oysters and liquor in a blender or food processor until a smooth paste is achieved.

3. In a separate medium saucepan, add the oyster purée, soy sauce, sugar, salt, and molasses. Simmer for 20 minutes over low heat.

4. Mix the flour with the water in a small bowl and blend. Add the mixture to the oyster sauce and stir until thick. Simmer over very low heat for an additional 10 minutes; do not boil.

5. Use the sauce on the spot or bottle it and store in the refrigerator for up to one week.

Hollandaise Sauce

This buttery smooth sauce proves that life can be beautiful. The calories slide down so easily, don't even bother counting them!

Makes 1 cup

1/2 cup (1 stick) butter, cut into 3 equal parts
3 large egg yolks
Dash of salt
Dash of cayenne pepper
2 tablespoons lemon juice, or more to taste

1. Put water in the bottom of a double boiler, making sure it does not touch the bottom of the top part. Over low heat, heat the water but do not boil.

2. Place the egg yolks and one-third of the butter in the top part of the double boiler. Stir continuously with a wooden spoon until the butter melts. Add another third of butter and stir until melted. Add the remaining butter and continue to stir, preventing the eggs from cooking.

3. Add the salt, cayenne pepper, and lemon juice and stir until thick. If the heat is too high, the sauce will curdle. If the sauce starts to separate, add 1 tablespoon cold water and whisk rapidly.

4. When the sauce is thickened, remove the top from the bottom boiler and set aside. Do not try to reheat, as it is perfectly proper to serve Hollandaise sauce warm or at room temperature. The sauce can be kept warm by placing the pan in one inch of warm water until ready to use. If the sauce has become dry, simply add a tablespoon of warm water and whisk.

Shoalwater Tartar Sauce

Fresh tartar sauce is truly worth making, as there is no comparison with the bottled varieties. It also doubles and stores easily, so you don't have to make it from scratch every time. Serve with oyster sandwich recipes, and always have a creamy bowl on the table when serving fried oysters. For a variation, omit the green olives and add capers.

Makes 1 1/2 cups

1 cup mayonnaise (preferably homemade)
1 scallion, finely chopped
1 teaspoon Dijon mustard
1/4 cup pitted green olives, finely chopped
1 tablespoon lemon juice
1/2 teaspoon finely minced garlic
2 tablespoons minced fresh parsley
2 tablespoons pickle relish
1 tablespoon green olive juice

1. Combine all the ingredients in a medium bowl and mix well. Taste for seasonings and adjust as needed. More lemon juice may be added for that extra tangy flavor.

2. Use at once or bottle and store in refrigerator for up to one week.

*Oyster, dear to the gourmet, beneficent Oyster,
exciting rather than sating, all stomachs digest you.
All stomachs bless you!*
—Seneca

Shoalwater Cocktail Sauce

Feel free to experiment with the measurements in this recipe; some like it hot and spicy while others like a more mild taste. Regardless of what you prefer, this is an excellent sauce that really brightens a meal.

Makes 1 cup

1 cup unseasoned canned tomato sauce
1 teaspoon horseradish
1 teaspoon lemon juice, or more to taste
Dash of Worcestershire sauce
Dash of hot pepper sauce, such as Tabasco
Dash of onion powder or 1 teaspoon finely minced onion
1 tablespoon soy sauce or Teriyaki sauce
1/2 teaspoon minced garlic
Dash of celery salt
Freshly ground black pepper

In a medium bowl, combine all the ingredients and mix well. Let sit for an hour before serving, if possible. Store any leftover sauce in the refrigerator for up to one week

Digestion is the business of the stomach and indigestion that of the doctors.
—L'Almanach des Gourmands, 1803
Grimod de la Reynière

The Walrus and the Carpenter

by Lewis Carroll, 1872

"The sun was shining on the sea,
Shining with all his might:
He did his very best to make
The billows smooth and bright—
And this was odd, because it was
The middle of the night.

The moon was shining sulkily,
Because she thought the sun
Had got no business to be there
After the day was done—
"It's very rude of him," she said,
"To come and spoil the fun!"

The sea was wet as wet could be,
The sands were dry as dry.
You could not see a cloud, because
No cloud was in the sky:
No birds were flying overhead—
There were no birds to fly.

The Walrus and the Carpenter
Were walking close at hand;
They wept like anything to see
Such quantities of sand:
"If this were only cleared away,"
They said, "it would be grand!"

"If seven maids with seven mops
Swept it for half a year,
Do you suppose," the Walrus said,
"That they could get it clear?"

"I doubt it," said the Carpenter.
And shed a bitter tear.

"O Oysters, come and walk with us!"
The Walrus did beseech.
"A pleasant walk, a pleasant talk.
Along the briny beach:
We cannot do with more than four.
To give a hand to each."

The eldest Oyster looked at him.
But never a word he said:
The eldest Oyster winked his eye.
And shook his heavy head—
Meaning to say he did not choose
To leave the oyster-bed.

But four young Oysters hurried up,
All eager for the treat:
Their coats were brushed, their faces washed,
Their shoes were clean and neat—
And this was odd, because, you know,
They hadn't any feet.

Four other Oysters followed them,
And yet another four;
And thick and fast they came at last,
And more, and more, and more—
All hopping through the frothy waves.
And scrambling to the shore.

The Walrus and the Carpenter
Walked on a mile or so,
And then they rested on a rock
Conveniently low:
And all the little Oysters stood
And waited in a row.

"The time has come," the Walrus said,
"To talk of many things:
Of shoes—and ships—and sealing
  wax—
Of cabbages—and kings.
And why the sea is boiling hot—
And whether pigs have wings."

"But wait a bit," the Oysters cried,
"Before we have our chat;
For some of us are out of breath,
And all of us are fat!"
"No hurry!" said the Carpenter.
They thanked him much for that.

"A loaf of bread," the Walrus said,
"Is what we chiefly need:
Pepper and vinegar besides
Are very good indeed—
Now, if you're ready, Oysters dear,
We can begin to feed."

"But not on us!" the Oysters cried.
Turning a little blue.
"After such kindness, that
  would be
A dismal thing to do!"
"The night is fine," the Walrus said.
"Do you admire the view?"

"It was so kind of you to come!
And you are very nice!"
The Carpenter said nothing but
"Cut us another slice:
I wish you were not quite so deaf—
I've had to ask you twice."

"It seems a shame," the Walrus said,
"To play them such a trick.
After we've brought them out so far,
And made them trot so quick!"
The Carpenter said nothing but
"The butter's spread too thick!"

"I weep for you," the Walrus said:
"I deeply sympathize."
With sobs and tears he sorted out
Those of the largest size.
Holding his pocket handkerchief
Before his streaming eyes.

"O Oysters," said the Carpenter,
"You've had a pleasant run!
Shall we be trotting home again?"
But answer came there none—
And this was scarcely odd, because
They'd eaten every one.

Basic Vinaigrette Salad Dressing

While studying under James Beard at his cooking school in Gearhart, Oregon, I was required to make vinaigrette salad dressing. I passed my dressing around the table with the dressings my classmates had made, and even though vinaigrette basically consists of oil, vinegar, and herbs, all 30 concoctions were very different. The cause of this difference is the many flavored vinegars available—herb, fruit, wine—as well as a variety of oils and herbs. I have listed the proportions I like to use and some of my favorite variations, though you will be the best one to determine the final construction of your signature dressing.

Makes 1/2 cup

8 tablespoons oil
2 tablespoons vinegar
1 tablespoon herbs (preferably fresh) per cup of dressing

Variations:

Sweet accent: Use white balsamic vinegar, raspberry, or other fruit-flavored vinegars with a sweet herb, such as rosemary, tarragon, or thyme, and a light oil.

Garlic accent: Mix good olive oil, wine-flavored vinegar, and a pinch of oregano, thyme, and freshly ground black pepper. Finely mince 1 garlic clove. Mix all the ingredients and let stand 5 minutes before serving.

Lemon accent: Substitute fresh lemon juice for the vinegar portion.

Creamy accent: Add a little plain yogurt, heavy cream, mustard, or mayonnaise and mix well.

Anchovy accent: Mash a few small anchovy fillets and add them to a dressing made with olive oil, garlic, oregano, basil, freshly ground black pepper, and fresh lemon juice. For a thicker consistency, add a coddled egg (page 172). Mix thoroughly before serving.

Life is so brief that we should not glance either too far backwards or forwards in order to be happy. Let us therefore study how to fix our happiness in our glass and on our plate.
—*Almanach des Gourmands, 1803*
Grimod de La Reyniere

Garlic Butter Sauce

This sauce is perfect for dipping or sautéing. Dunk fire-baked oysters, chunks of sourdough bread, steamer clams, or anything else you have! Although it is potent, it is this feature that complements the delicate flavor of oysters so well. A variation using fresh herbs follows.

Makes 1/3 cup

1/2 cup (1 stick) butter, melted
1 tablespoon lemon juice, or more to taste
1 to 1 1/2 teaspoons finely minced garlic
Freshly ground black pepper

1. In a small saucepan, melt the butter over low heat. Clarify the butter by removing any foam that rises to the top.

2. Add the lemon juice, garlic, and black pepper and continue cooking over low heat. Be careful not to brown the garlic, as garlic tends to become bitter if allowed to brown. Serve hot. Butter sauces may be stored in the refrigerator for up to one week.

Garlic Butter Sauce with Herbs: Add 1 tablespoon fresh fennel fronds, finely chopped, or other chopped fresh herbs to step 2 when making Garlic Butter Sauce. Complete the recipe as directed.

Soy-Mirin Sauce

*A favorite among many, this sauce is excellent when
served with steamed or fire-baked oysters. It can also
be used as a marinade for other types of fish.*

Soy sauce
Mirin (Japanese rice wine)
Chili oil

1. Mix one part soy sauce with two parts Mirin (Japanese rice wine) in a medium bowl. Add a few drops of chili oil, adjusting the hotness to your preferences.

2. Place the sauce in a jar and shake thoroughly. Use immediately. This sauce is best made fresh for each use.

*We eat nothing without smelling it with more or less
consciousness; and for unknown foods the nose acts always
as a sentinel, and cries, "Who goes there?"*
—Jean Anthelme Brillat-Savarin

Considering the Oyster

The Fate of the Oyster

In 1850, the native beds of oysters, several feet thick, were heavily harvested for forty years and nothing was done to help them replenish themselves.

By 1864, almost all of the mature marketable oysters on Shoalwater Bay's natural beds had been harvested. The peak year for the native oyster industry was 1891. More than 131 thousand bushels of oysters were sold.

In 1894, the U.S. Fish Commission imported 88 barrels of east coast oysters to Shoalwater Bay by railroad and proved that small oysters from the east coast could be successfully grown locally and marketed in west coast cities.

Between 1902 and 1912, 360 railroad coaches, each filled with barrels of young eastern oysters, were sent to Willapa Harbor. Prices for the mature were high, but the profits were minimal because of transportation costs and labor.

By 1919, the remaining eastern oysters and the native oyster were almost completely exterminated by the red tide (a marine plankton) that year. The death of both industries caused the bay to become quiet. The processing plants and equipment became useless major investments.

Professor Trevor Kincaid, noted zoologist of the University of Washington, had long been acquainted with the oyster industry of the state; he knew Willapa Bay and was cognizant of the fine oysters grown along the Japanese coast. He began talking with Gerard T. Morgan, a Seattle lawyer, who became interested and endeavored to buy all county-owned tidelands and whatever land was suitable for oyster culture. He started several stock companies and made plantings of Japanese seed oysters. The oysters did well. The new industry grew, with an increasing number of companies and individuals participating. From the original planting of 40 boxes of seed oysters in 1928, plantings reached 50 thousand cases in 1935 and continued until the outbreak of World War II, when seed from Japan became unavailable for six years. There was a massive catch of oysters in the bay in 1941. This was extremely fortunate, in that it furnished oysters that carried the industry through the war years. Again the oysters were over-harvested and the situation changed. Oysters fattened in only a few places, and transplanting became necessary.

Science and technology have once again brought the oyster into the limelight. Hatcheries now produce oyster larvae and oyster farmers are able to purchase seed. Along with the many large commercial growers, "hobby" farmers are also providing us with the delectable bivalve for all to enjoy.

Nutritional Facts

The benefits of eating oysters have been known for hundreds of years. Rich in omega-3 fatty acids, oysters are believed to be instrumental in the development and function of the brain, retinas, and sperm. They've been attributed to such qualities as curing goiter, cleansing the skin, and even improving your sex life.

M. F. K. Fisher writes in her book, *Consider the Oyster*: "There is an astounding number of men, and some of them have graduated from Yale and even Princeton, who know positively that oysters are an aphrodisiac...one of the best. They can tell of countless chaps whose powers have been increased nigh unto the billy goat's simply from eating raw, cold oysters."

Seriously, oysters are one of the purest forms of food on the planet. They contain the chemical elements oxygen, hydrogen, and nitrogen, and are high in the content of iron, copper, zinc, and vitamin B-12. Furthermore, they're high in phosphorus, which is considered "brain food" by many reputable scientists.

It's been noted in books long before the fifteenth century that people ate oysters to aid their intellects. In *The Art of Eating*, another book by M. F. K. Fisher, she writes "...somewhere after 1461, Louis XI made it obligatory for the group of great men he gathered to him in his reign, to swallow a certain amount of such easy phosphorus each day." Even traditional Chinese medicine uses the oyster shell as a relief for insomnia, dizziness, blurred vision, and hypertension.

A delicacy that is as healthy as it is delicious—the world has no choice but to enjoy!

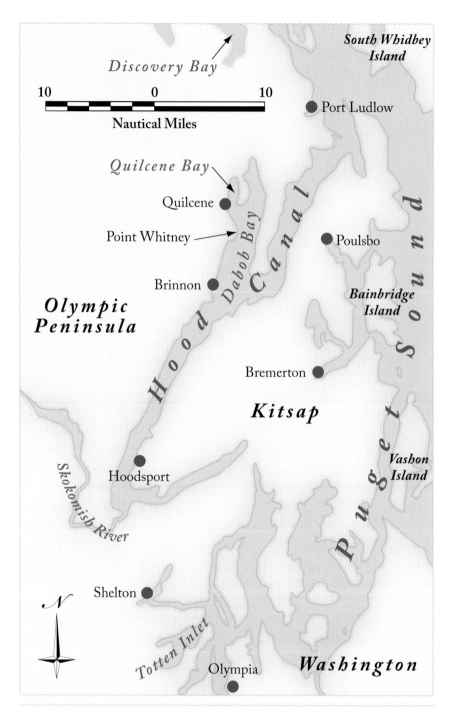

Discovery Bay

South Whidbey
Island

10 0 10

Nautical Miles

Port Ludlow

Quilcene Bay

Quilcene

Point Whitney

Dabob Bay

Poulsbo

Brinnon

Hood Canal

*Olympic
Peninsula*

*Bainbridge
Island*

Bremerton

Kitsap

Puget Sound

*Vashon
Island*

Skokomish River

Hoodsport

N

Shelton

Olympia

Totten Inlet

Washington

Oyster Vintage

When pondering the subject of how to describe the various species and varieties of oysters, the analogy of wine tasting comes to mind. Just as there are many varietals within a single wine growing region, each with its own distinct flavor depending on the soil content and weather, each variety of oyster has a distinct flavor according to its environment. For example, some are more saline in flavor, while others have a higher mineral content delivering a slightly more metallic taste. Those with a muddier taste most likely spent their life on a silty bottom compared to those grown suspended on long lines or in trays, which gives them a cleaner taste.

The West Coast could just as easily be called oyster country as it is wine country. There are more than fifty different varieties of oysters in the Pacific Northwest region, which derive from the Pacific oyster. Other species grown in the Northwest are the European Flat, Eastern, Olympia (the only native oyster) and the Kumamoto.

Eastern Oyster (*Crassostrea virginica*)
Sometimes known as the Gulf or Atlantic oyster, the Eastern oyster was introduced to the West Coast from the East Coast when the local supply of oysters was depleted in the early 1900s. It takes longer to mature and is not commercially grown on a large scale. The meat is creamy white with a sweet mineral taste, and its larger shell tends to be smooth and elongated.

Variety:
Totten Virginica (Totten Inlet, Puget Sound, Washington)

European Flat Oyster (*Ostrea edulis*)
Originally from Europe, this oyster is commercially grown in the
Puget Sound on a small scale. The shell is very smooth and flat and
does not have a deep cup like the Pacific oyster or Kumamoto oyster.
Slightly metallic in taste, it is similar to the Belon of France. Coppery
in color, it does not have the typical black-velvet rim of the Pacific
oyster surrounding its creamy white meat. The European oyster is best
consumed raw on the half shell.

Varieties:
Discovery Bay Flats (North Puget Sound, Washington)
Snow Creek (Discovery Bay, Port Angeles, Washington)
Totten and Samish Flat (South Puget Sound, Shelton, Washington)
Westcott Bay Euro-Flats (San Juan Islands, Washington)

Kumamoto Oyster (*Crassostrea sikamea*)
Originally from Japan, the Kumamoto oyster is very small and is similar
to the Pacific oyster, with a deeply cupped and rough-edged shell. Its
velvet black-rimmed meat is plump, sweet, and delicate, but few growers
have succeeded in cultivating it. These oysters are found in Willapa Bay
and the Puget Sound and can only be reproduced in a hatchery.

Varieties:
Chapman Kumo (South Puget Sound, Shelton, Washington)
Totten Kumo (South Puget Sound, Shelton, Washington
Willapa (Willapa Bay, Southwest Washington)

Olympia Oyster (*Ostrea conchaphila*)
This is the only oyster native to the Pacific Coast and is found in
the waters from Baja, California, to Sitka, Alaska. In the Pacific
Northwest it lives in areas around Olympia, Shelton, and Willapa Bay.

Very small in size (about the size of a quarter), its shell is gnarled and blueish-gray-purple. Its edges are smooth, unlike the rough edges of the Pacific oyster, and its slightly metallic or coppery aftertaste is its most distinguishing characteristic.

The maps on pages 19 and 164 shows where the many varieties of oysters are grown.

Pacific Oyster (*Crassostsrea gigas*)

The Pacific oyster totals 99-percent of U.S. West Coast production and is one of the most intensively cultivated oyster species in the world. Originally from Japan, it has a distinctive black-velvet rim around its meat, tasting sweet and rich with a slight hint of cucumber in the finish. Growing up to four inches or larger, its shell is deeply cupped and becomes its own baking dish. Pacifics will vary slightly in taste according to the different regions from which they come. These larger varieties are best for cooking and barbecuing.

Varieties:
Barron Point (Skookum Inlet, South Puget Sound, Washington)
Dabob (Dabob Bay, Quilcene, Washington)
Evening Cove (Vancouver Island, BC)
Fanny Bay (Bayes Sound, Vancouver Island, BC)
Gold Creek (South Puget Sound, Washington)
Hamma-Hamma (South Hood Canal, Washington)
Pearl Point (North Oregon Coast)
Penn Cove (Whidby Island, Washington)
Quilcene (Quilcene, Washington)
Totten Pacific (Totten Inlet, South Puget Sound, Shelton, Washington)
Westcott (Westcott Point, San Juan Islands, Washington)
Willapa (Willapa Bay, Oysterville, Washington)
Yaquina (Yaquina Bay, North Oregon Coast)

The Life of an Oyster

Seeding

This is the process of collecting baby oysters (spat), which attach to oyster shells (cultch). This is done naturally by Mother Nature or can be done artificially in the hatchery. Oysters begin their life as free swimming larvae, and after about three weeks, they attach to available cultch (such as the oyster shell) to begin their sedentary lives. Reproduction usually occurs in the warmer months, and because this natural method is not always dependable, oyster growers have gone to tank culture as opposed to letting Mother Nature handle it. Tank culture is a more controlled method of obtaining seed. This is done in a hatchery where adult oysters are spawned and the larvae are collected. These larvae are then grown in large seawater tanks and fed algae, also grown in the hatchery. Within a few weeks they are ready to begin metamorphosis and attach to available cultch material. This cultch material is placed in another seawater tank to which the larvae are added. Again, the spat must be fed until they are eventually moved out to the natural beds.

Growing

There are two ways of growing spat to maturity: bottom culture and off-bottom culture. For bottom culture, growers will scatter seed (baby oysters) over the bottom of the oyster bed of rock, mud, or sand. For off-bottom culture, growers will float seed strung on lines, hung on racks, or placed in trays. There are many individual methods of rigging off-bottom culture. A prospective oyster grower will choose between types of culture depending on the environment and preference.

Harvesting

Harvesting oysters can be done any number of ways. Regardless of method, it is backbreaking work controlled by the tides and the weather. Some popular modern techniques involve dredging at high tide and hand picking at low tide. In the past, they were often collected with tongs or rakes.

Marketing

Like the many creative recipes in this book, marketing oysters is equally versatile. To date, they are sold fresh in the shell, shucked, processed in jars or cans, and smoked.

Did you know?
In the spring of 1854, John S. Morgan and friends formed a
company that would include all phases of the oyster business.
They proposed to collect oysters and have their own ships carry
their oysters to market and bring back supplies for themselves
and others. By 1870, six other companies had been formed.
Books were kept for the oystermen by these companies with a
debit and a credit side so, as Charles Stevens said, "Oysters are
legal tender here with all kinds of dealing out of stores." Actual
money did not change hands.

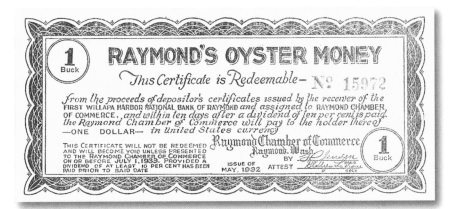

Raymond's "Oyster money" issue of May 1932

Glossary of Cooking Terms, Methods, and Equipment

Beurre manié: The mixing of 2 parts flour to 3 parts softened butter kneaded together to be used as a thickening agent. Use your finger to knead the softened butter and flour until combined. Form pea-size balls, then add a few at a time to hot liquid, stirring after each addition. Keep extra balls covered and in the freezer for future use, when a thickening agent is quickly needed at the last minute.

Coddle: To coddle an egg, bring water to a boil in a small sauce pan, then remove from heat. Take 1 egg in the shell and steep in hot water for 3 minutes. Remove egg from pan and run under cold water to stop cooking. Crack shell and use immediately.

Double boiler: This is a double saucepan. The bottom is used for heating the top with simmering water. The water level should never touch the bottom of the top part. Use a double boiler when making delicate sauces, such as Hollandaise, a white sauce, or when egg yolks are used as a thickening agent.

Garlic: Skin garlic by lightly smashing the clove with the flat side of a knife. This breaks the skin, which then comes off with ease.

Marinade: The liquid—usually of wine, herbs, and spices— in which oysters and other foods steep in order to take on the flavors of the mixture.

Marinate: To let stand in the marinade.

Oyster liquor: The oyster's natural water or juice, contained in the shell or jar.

Poach: To cook slowly over low heat in a small amount of liquid, such as water, oyster liquor, wine, or broth.

Purée: To make a smooth paste of ingredients by putting in a blender or rubbing through a fine-mesh strainer.

Roux: A blending of oil and flour that is cooked over low heat until light brown in color and smoky in aroma. It is used as a flavor base and thickener in soups and sauces.

Sauté: To cook in a skillet over medium heat in a small amount of butter or oil.

Steep: To immerse in liquid.

Zest: The strongly flavored and colored outer part (rind) of citrus fruits like lemons, limes, and oranges. Do not include the white pith when using, as it does not have any flavor and is bitter.

Recipe Index

Acknowledgments

I wish to express more than the usual acknowledgments to those who aided in the creation of this book.

At the end of a delightful evening spent with congenial friends and superbly prepared food, I always thanked my guests for their honesty and support.

I would like to thank the following list of tasters:

> Katherine and Paul Calvert
> Cassin Espy
> The late "Uncle" Cecil Espy
> Chris and David Jensen
> John Speziali
> Michael Ware
> Larry Warnberg
> Marge Welling
> Carlos Welsh

And a big THANK YOU to all those people whose encouraging words about this project kept me inspired. And finally, a special thank you to my husband/manager Carlos. Without his support and never-ending patience, this project would have been abandoned.